SOCIAL WORK PLACEMENTS

Placements can be one of the most exciting parts of your social work training but also one of the most daunting. This rough guide will help you to make the most of your practice learning opportunities, as well as anticipating some of the problem areas and pitfalls to avoid. It covers:

➢ Preparing for your placement
➢ Getting to grips with placement documentation
➢ Understanding how and what you might learn on placement
➢ Integrating theory with practice
➢ Non-traditional placements
➢ Anticipating difficulties and dealing with them
➢ Getting the best from assessment and evaluation.

Using a cast of 'fellow travellers' – students, work-based supervisors, practice educators and college tutors – to illustrate issues raised, the guide is accessible and contains plenty of case studies. It is the ideal book for anyone wanting to make sure their placement goes as well as possible, whether they are a student or a supervisor.

Professor Mark Doel is Research Professor of Social Work in the Centre for Health and Social Care Research at Sheffield Hallam University, UK. He is also the author and co-author of *Educating Professionals: practice learning in health and social care*, *Experiencing Social Work: learning from service users*, *Using Groupwork*, *The Task-Centred Book*, *Practice Learning and Teaching*, *The Essential Groupworker* and *Modern Social Work Practice*.

STUDENT SOCIAL WORK

This exciting new textbook series is ideal for all students studying to be qualified social workers, whether at undergraduate or masters level. Covering key elements of the social work curriculum, the books are accessible, interactive and thought-provoking.

NEW TITLES

Human Growth and Development
John Sudbery

Mental Health Social Work in Context
Nick Gould

Social Work and Social Policy
Jonathan Dickens

Social Work Placements
Mark Doel

FORTHCOMING TITLES

Integrating Social Work Theory and Practice
Pam Green Lister

Social Work
A reader
Vivienne E. Cree

Building Relationships and Communicating with Young Children
A practical guide
Karen Winter

SOCIAL WORK

PLACEMENTS

A TRAVELLER'S GUIDE

MARK DOEL

Routledge
Taylor & Francis Group

LONDON AND NEW YORK

First published 2010 by Routledge
2 Park Square, Milton Park, Abingdon, Oxon, OX14 4RN
Simultaneously published in the USA and Canada
by Routledge
270 Madison Avenue, New York, NY 10016

Routledge is an imprint of the Taylor & Francis Group, an informa business

Typeset in Frutiger by
Saxon Graphics Ltd
Printed and bound in Great Britain by
TJ International Ltd, Padstow, Cornwall

British Library Cataloguing in Publication Data
A catalogue record for this book is available from the British Library

Library of Congress Cataloging-in-Publication Data
Doel, Mark.
   Social work placements : a traveller's guide / Mark Doel.
        p. cm.
   1. Social workers—Training of. 2. Social service—Practice. 3. Social service—
Vocational guidance. I. Title.
   HV40.D633 2010
   361.3071'55—dc22   2009025792

ISBN10: 0-415-49911-9 (hbk)
ISBN10: 0-415-49912-7 (pbk)
ISBN10: 0-203-86240-6 (ebk)

ISBN13: 978-0-415-49911-8 (hbk)
ISBN13: 978-0-415-49912-5 (pbk)
ISBN13: 978-0-203-86240-7 (ebk)

DEDICATION

This book is dedicated to the memory of David Sawdon (1942–2008). David's contribution to our knowledge and understanding of practice education is enormous. He was tutor for all three of my own placements as a student. I got to know him as a friend and colleague and he is greatly missed.

CONTENTS

PART ONE   BASICS   01

PART TWO   THE GUIDE   13

● CHAPTER 1: DOCUMENTATION 15–36

● CHAPTER 2: ARRIVING 37–53

CHARTS

BLOGS

TOURS

SYMBOLS

IN THE GUIDE

- ⛽ assistance
- 💬 blog
- 📚 books and articles
- ⚡ detour; rethink
- 🐕 *2 Doors* blog
- ▷ direction to related topic
- 🗁 documentation
- ⊠ downloads
- 👁 eye witness
- () feedback
- ⚲ findings / discovery
- ⓘ information / briefings
- ✛ map; orientation
- 💣 problem
- 🗐 rehearsal
- ⧗ time and deadlines
- ✂ tips
- ✘ toolkit and accessories
- ❧ tour
- ⛩ trap
- ⚇ visa; rewards
- **W** website link

IN SOCIALWORKLAND

- ⤙ airport
- ⚑ battle
-)(bridge
- ✠ castle of hard knocks
- ▣ city
- ✳ communication crossroads
- 🏭 factory of policies and procedures
- ♠ forest
- ϒ fountain
- 🏛 gallery of styles
- ✿ gardens
- ✸ incinerator (burn-out)
- ⌇ levels
- ⟋ mast
- ≋ meadow
- ▬ mist
- 🏚 multiprofessional house
- ♧ orchard; wood
- .···· path; trail
- ⬭ pool (for reflection)
- .—·· railway – logical thinking line
- ⚱ retreat (study time retreat centre)
- ⤳ river
- ⬥ road of professional identity
- ⓘ service user expertise
- 🏰 stadium of competence
- ═ swamp
- ☠ tarpits of reorganisation
- 🗐 theatre of rehearsal
- 🕘 time management
- ● town
- 🜂 well of supervision

> agency
> territory

NB An earlier version of *Socialworkland* appeared in Doel, M. and Shardlow, S.M. (eds) (1996), *Social Work in a Changing World: An International Perspective on Practice Learning*, Aldershot: Arena.

ACKNOWLEDGEMENTS

With so many friends and colleagues in social work practice learning it is difficult to know where to begin to acknowledge all the influences that have shaped the thinking and passion for placements that inspired this book. I remember my own supervisors and placement tutor very well, despite the passing of well over three decades. The students I supervised over two decades also taught me much about good practice in supervision (and what not to do, too) as have those 'students' I have mentored and worked with during workshops for the Practice Teaching Award. Membership of the National Organisation of Practice Teachers (NOPT) and invitations to practice teachers' training groups continue to provide regular enthusiasm and encouragement from like-minded colleagues who see placement learning and teaching as part of their professional life blood.

Although I have sole responsibility for this book, I would like to take this opportunity to thank past writing partners from whom I have learned much, in particular Peter Marsh, Steven Shardlow, Catherine Sawdon, David Sawdon and Lesley Best. Over the years, and more especially in recent times, I have been fortunate to be able to research many aspects of placements and I would like to thank my research colleagues, especially Debbie Develin, Elaine Flynn, Dave Henry, Anne Hollows, Jane McLenachan, Caroline Mulrooney, Pete Nelson, Hilary Pengelly and Janet Williams. The research would not have been possible without the support of colleagues from the (then) Practice Learning Taskforce and Skills for Care, in particular Cheryl Wall, Carol Holloway and Nasreen Hammond and, of course, all those students, practice teachers, development workers and service user educators who, over the years, have taken the trouble to respond to my questionnaires, even when life is very hectic. I have tried to bring all of these experiences to life in the book.

It has been fun writing this book. My hope is that the fun I had writing it is not at the expense of the reader's enjoyment. So I would like to thank Grace McInnes, Commissioning Editor at Routledge, for encouraging me to pursue the idea of the travel guide, Khanam Virjee and Nick Ascroft for their regular check-ins with me and help with the website that accompanies the guide (and you tried your best, Khanam, to persuade the holders of the 'Rough Guide' title to allow us to use it!) and Rob Brown for his able project management of the book.

Pete Nelson and Sandy Fraser provided very valuable feedback and suggestions as readers of the text as it developed. My thanks to them both for pointing to areas that I had overlooked and for their enthusiasm for the project. Pete was one of my former students on placement in Sheffield Family and Community Services Department, so things have come full circle. I am indebted to Beverley Murphy and Elaine Flynn for their help in compiling the documents for the website that accompanies this guide and, indeed, to my colleagues at Sheffield Hallam University for the use of these illustrative materials.

Last and not least, my sincere thanks to Jan, who always knew what I was up to when I went slinking off to write a few more paragraphs, but never complained – even when we were supposed to be on holiday.

INTRODUCTION

Ask a social worker of some years' experience what they remember about their professional training and it is highly likely they will talk about their placements. No matter how interesting or challenging the classwork has been, it is the opportunity to experience social work directly in a practice setting that has the potential to inspire and to stay in the memory.

The placement is the opportunity for learning with real people in practice. It is a chance to have hands-on teaching and supervision on a one-to-one basis. Of course, placements have their stresses, too. They are not easy to obtain and you may find yourself in a placement that you have not chosen or that has had to be arranged at the last minute. Your learning and practice is assessed, and this can make you anxious, wondering what standards are expected and whether you are meeting them. Is the placement going to offer you the necessary opportunities? All in all, the placement is likely to be both an exciting and a challenging experience.

The nature of placements is changing in response to the pressure for more of them. Placements in settings that are 'not social work' are increasingly common. These *non-traditional placements* can offer interesting opportunities for learning, but proper safeguards should be in place to ensure that the experiences in these practice sites can be translated into social work learning. There are similar challenges for placements in students' own workplaces, to make sure that they are transformed from a workplace to a placement.

If you are providing a placement or thinking of developing placements, students can bring a new outlook and a fresh challenge to you, your team and the agency. Supervising a student is a good way to reflect on your own practice, to subject it to scrutiny, and to help your agency to develop as a learning organisation. Students should not be used as extra staff, but they can legitimately support and develop new work or projects that might not be possible without them. Practice learning can also have a positive impact on recruitment; students and agencies get to know one another and what is now a placement can later turn into an employment. Staff can find that supervising students is a good way to continue their professional development and, for the agency at large, practice learning may be an opportunity to enhance staff morale and therefore improve staff retention. Placements are not just about offering individual students an opportunity for practice learning; they are about a wider philosophy that links practice agencies to higher education, research and continuing professional development.

Placements can have their stresses for supervisors and the agencies that provide them. The responsibility of offering a placement, and the supervision and assessment that goes with it, is considerable. In most circumstances the student brings much of value to the placement, but there are occasions when a student who is failing or at the margins can be a very real challenge, practically and emotionally.

For all these reasons and more, there is a pressing need for a guide to placements. The idea of the placement as a journey, at times exhilarating and at times challenging, is one that has inspired the metaphor for the book – as a travel guide to placements rather than a list of do's and dont's. The sense of excitement and apprehension that is experienced before a journey to a new land is similar to the experience of a placement, and the guiding and visiting relationship that characterises supervisor and student is much like the host's relationship to the guest. In this guide we have developed the notion of *Socialworkland*, an abstract idea but given a physical representation in the form of a map and elaborated through the book, with the hope that it throws a different kind of light on placements and adds to the reader's overall enjoyment. There are plenty of ways to develop the metaphor if the muse takes you; for example, by considering what your personal 'World Heritage site' would be in *Socialworkland*.

Along the way you will be introduced to *charts* which map specific aspects of the journey in more detail, and regular *blogs* written by fellow-travellers. These people – students, supervisors and the like – are introduced in *The Basics* (▷09). You will hear from them all, from time to time, as they reflect on their own experiences of placements, from different points of view. Occasionally, you will read two parallel stories in which the same person chooses one of two doors to enter, and you will learn about the different consequences of each of these choices. You are also invited on the occasional *tour*, a small excursion into an exercise or activity that goes into a particular topic in more depth. The guide points to further materials and examples of placement documents (indicated by ▷**W**). These can be downloaded at: www.routledge.com/textbooks/9780415499125

The book is written in an informal style, as befits a guide; 'you' might be the student or the supervisor, or some other traveller as fits the context. Though there is an effort to avoid acronyms, the language of placement can be confusing, so turn to the *Language* section in *Contexts* (▷226) when you need to. The guide uses the simple terms 'placement' and 'supervisor' but, as the Language section expounds, there is a history and a context to these words.

Referencing is relatively light, with significant and relevant texts and websites at the end of each chapter and further reading in *Contexts* (▷228). However, do not take this as an indication that the guide neglects theoretical underpinnings or the growing knowledge from research about practice learning. The guide is based on the current state of our knowledge of practice education, presented relatively casually and in ways that are designed to make this knowledge accessible, practical and interesting to the reader. I hope the guide achieves at least some of this aim.

All names of individuals and of organisations are fictitious and any persons or agencies with these names are entirely coincidental.

Mark Doel
Sheffield 2009

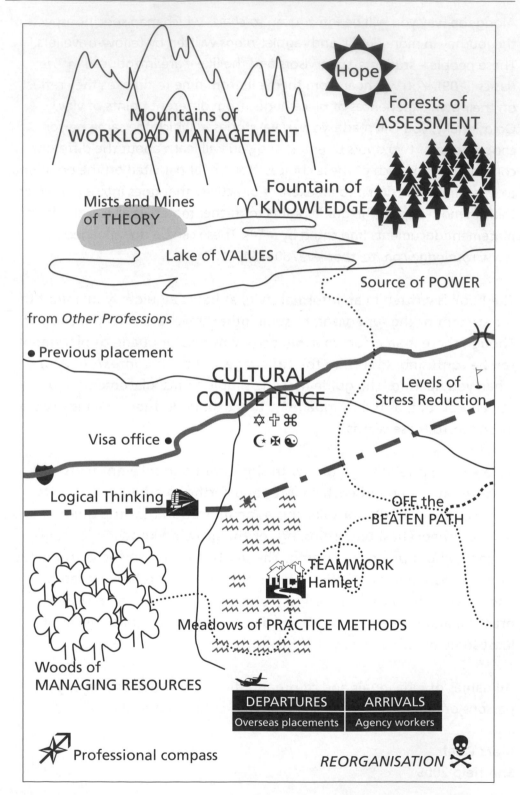

MAP OF *SOCIALWORKLAND*

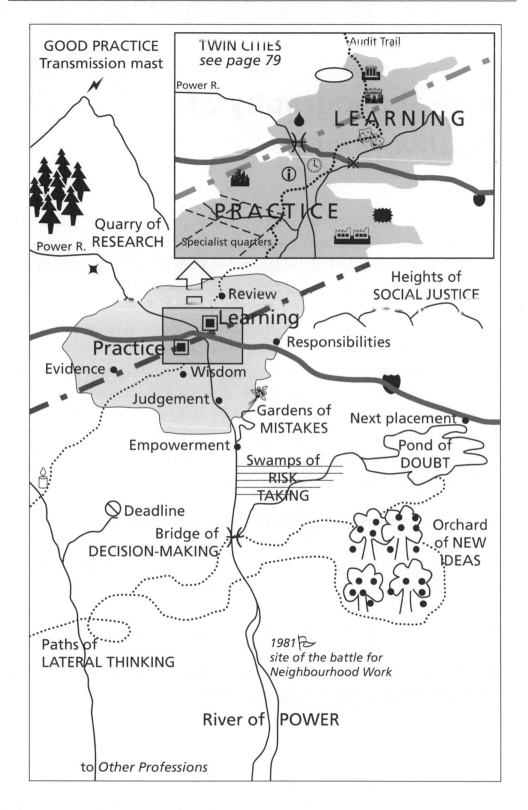

GOOD PRACTICE
Transmission mast

TWIN CITIES
see page 79

Power R.

LEARNING

PRACTICE

Quarry of
RESEARCH

Power R.

Specialist quarters

Heights of
SOCIAL JUSTICE

Review

Learning

Practice

Responsibilities

Evidence

Wisdom

Judgement

Gardens of
MISTAKES

Next placement

Empowerment

Pond of
DOUBT

Swamps of
RISK
TAKING

Deadline

Orchard
of NEW
IDEAS

Bridge of
DECISION-MAKING

Paths of
LATERAL THINKING

1981
site of the battle for
Neighbourhood Work

River of POWER

to *Other Professions*

Political geography of *Socialworkland*

The landscape of *Socialworkland* has a political geography that students should learn about during their travels. For example, is this a landscape that is being well-managed and resourced or does it face degradation and erosion? Who 'owns' the land? Is it a collective (and, if so, who are the partners?) or are there powerful landlords (and, if so, who are they?) Supervisors should consider their own understanding of this political geography and its relevance to the student's travels. The history of the land shapes the current topography and students need to discover past and alternative landscapes so they can critique the current one. There was a time and a place not so far away when probation officers would visit this landscape together with social workers; indeed, this is still the case in Scottish *Socialworkland*. Why are some lands lost or annexed elsewhere, such as *Probationland*?

If students are to develop a critical social work practice it is important that they have opportunities to learn about the political geography and the history of this landscape and to consider how it might change during their professional lifetimes and what influences there will be on these changes. What are the equivalences of 'climate change' in *Socialworkland* and how can future social workers be best equipped to look after their landscape?   Supervisors need to find time for these aspects of the student's travels, so they are not overlooked amidst the general busy-ness of rooting for evidence for occupational standards.

PART ONE

THE

BASICS

GETTING THERE

Social work students come to their courses via many different routes and in varied circumstances. The history of your journey to the course is likely, therefore, to influence the future journey to your placements. Have you just finished school or are you an older student? Someone who is studying for a first degree or a post-graduate? Studying in your home town or just arrived in a new city? Are you full time or part time on the course? Are you self-funding or sponsored by the agency in which you will also have a placement?

All of these different routes to the social work programme will suggest different possibilities for your placement journey. What every student has in common is the requirement to study for a minimum of 200 days in practice sites with at least two different service user groups, and to meet certain standards of practice and learning that will be assessed during their placement.

The guide that begins on page 13 will familiarise you with the details of all of these topics; for now, it is important that you think about what brought you to the course and how this will influence the shape, pattern and likely location of your placements.

SIMPLE RULES

To ensure that your journey to the placement is as successful as it can be, follow these three simple rules:

➤ Read the guidance that is provided for you by the social work programme in its *Course Handbook*; it pays to have a thorough understanding of this.
➤ Attend all the placement preparation sessions provided by the course; these will contain valuable advice to get you off to a good start. Don't rely on a friend to pass you the information.
➤ Complete all the documentation relating to your placement request promptly and conscientiously, making sure to keep appointments with your placement tutor.

RED TAPE

Documentation can be tedious but it is always important to deal with it promptly. When you are a qualified social worker you will have to handle red tape on behalf of service users to make sure they are well served, so start right now to show that you are capable of handling your own red tape, too.

READINESS

Documentation at the early stage of the course is likely to relate to readiness for learning, sometimes also called fitness for practice. Courses are required to test your readiness to commence a placement beforehand and each programme handles this in its own way. Make sure you are familiar with the procedures that your course uses and complete any paperwork that is asked of you (▷*Visa for practice learning* 43).

PLACEMENT FINDING

Some courses do not have a placement until the second year of study, whilst others have a placement early in the first year. If the latter, this means that you will be asked to complete a placement request quite soon and this will often be accompanied by an opportunity to discuss your placement interests with your personal tutor or a specific placement tutor. You might have definite views about what kind of placement you want and where you would like it to be, or you may be very uncertain at this point. Wherever you are on that line, talk things through with the tutor, using your placement finding form as a basis for the discussion (▷*Learning Agreement* 24).

Even if your placement is pretty much decided, perhaps because you are an employment-based student and your placement will be with your employer, it is always important to talk through the options with your tutor and make sure your preferences and concerns are noted in the documentation for *Placement finding* (▷38).

CRIMINAL RECORDS

The placement cannot go ahead without a Criminal Records Bureau (CRB) check; this is the equivalent of your passport so do nothing that might delay it (▷16).

HOURS AND HOLIDAYS

Placement expectations are often different from those that you have become used to at the university or college. You will usually be expected to be at the placement for the hours of work that employees at the practice site follow. If there are reasons why this should not or cannot be the case, discuss these very early on with your tutor so that the practice site can be asked what special arrangements might or might not be possible. Check in the handbook what the allowance for study time is and whether there is any holiday leave entitlement during the placement. Again, university terms often do not apply, and you are expected to follow the working days of the practice site. Always check and have the agreed hours and holidays recorded in the *Learning agreement* (▷24). Finally, if for religious reasons there are certain days or festivals that you wish to be excused from placement, it is very important that these are discussed in advance of placement finding and, ideally, as part of your application to the course.

CREDIT

If you are seeking credit for prior learning or experience make sure that you check this out well in advance; this will usually have been at the point at which you applied to come on the course or attended the selection process. Questions that need answers are whether your experience is sufficiently up to date and the mechanisms by which you will provide evidence of prior learning. You should be prepared for the fact that some of the procedures to provide evidence to back up your claim can be onerous, so much so that you may not feel like the credits have offered any relief from the full requirements.

CREDIT CHECK

There are many different kinds of credit with numerous acronyms:

- ➤ APEL (Accreditation of Prior Education and Learning)
- ➤ APCL (Accreditation of Prior Certified Learning)
- ➤ CATS (Credit Accumulation Transfer System)
- ➤ ECTS (European Credit Transfer System).

No credit can be given towards placements. (▷204 for more details)

CURRENCY

What are the financial arrangements for the placement? As a student, you do not receive any payment specific to your time on placement, nor do you have any extra fees for placements – though your bursary does include an element for travel to and from placement. You should check out arrangements for travel undertaken as part of your work for the placement – some sites reimburse but some do not (and some might pay for a bus pass).

For placement providers there are funds for practice learning which are provided centrally and channelled through each programme. A daily placement fee (DPF) is paid to placement providers, but you need to check how much this is, whether you receive all of it and how payments are organised. Payment for *off-site supervisors* (▷*Language* 228) usually comes out of the daily placement fee. In some agencies the on-site supervisor receives a direct payment (an honorarium). All of these arrangements need to be agreed and confirmed before a placement starts, including the financial arrangements for placements that are cut short or extended for whatever reasons.

PROBLEMS WITH TRAVELLING

The social work programme will have told you at various points (admission, preparation, placement-finding discussions) that travel to placements is always a likelihood. Placements are not thick on the ground and most programmes have to search a wide area to provide sufficient placements, in terms of quality and quantity. This is true of programmes that are situated in an urban setting, so do not assume that a city-based course might not involve placement travel.

The course will try its best to take account of your personal circumstances, especially if these have changed in ways that you could not have anticipated. Long-standing caring responsibilities that you were aware of when you applied to the course are not the same as sudden changes in life events. You need to be honest with the programme from the point of application about what is possible in terms of travel so you will not be disappointed later.

TRAVELLERS WITH DISABILITIES

Placements have a duty and responsibility to provide for all students who have been admitted to a social work programme regardless of age, ethnicity, gender, faith, disability, etc. Disability discrimination is illegal and placements are expected to make all reasonable adjustments to ensure that students with physical disabilities (such as wheelchair users) and learning difficulties (such as dyslexia) can be placed.

To help practice sites fulfil this, it is important that students, supervisors, tutors and agency managers work together to consider what the student's specific needs are and how the placement can best meet them. This is especially true of 'hidden' disabilities such as epilepsy, where it is important that placements know how to work with you to manage any potential medical emergencies.

Sites offering a placement to a student using a wheelchair might find this website useful:

http://www.wheelchairnet.org/ WCN_TownHall/Docs/etiquette.html

GAY *SOCIALWORKLAND*

As a gay, lesbian or bisexual student you should consider whether you want or need access to appropriate support groups and declare any requests, so that the prospective placement can assess whether such provision is likely to be available and, if not, what alternatives might be put in place.

ISOLATED TRAVELLERS

The placement is intended to be a rewarding, if challenging experience. However, it should not be isolating. What supports might you need and expect if, for example you find yourself the only person from a black and minority ethnic group travelling in this particular incarnation of *Socialworkland?* It is important to discuss this possibility and what kinds of support (outside the placement if necessary) will help you to counter potential isolation.

GROUP TOURS

There are indications that group placements are becoming more common, especially with the growth of placements in non-traditional settings (▷*Groups* 184 and ▷*Group guiding* 112). Whether you are on placement together with other students at the same practice site and/or experiencing group supervision, fellow students can be a valuable source of support and learning. Make sure that your individual needs will also be met; ▷*Learning agreement* 24 as a good place to discuss the balance of individual and group learning and support.

SPECIALIST DESTINATIONS

Though there are suggestions that parts of the social work qualification might start to specialise (⊠1), for now it is a generic one. This means that it qualifies you for social work in any setting. However, the practice of social work is now very largely in specialist settings – children and families, mental health, older adults, disabilities, criminal justice and the like. The placement provides a *context* for social work practice and the supervisor will help you make transitions between the specific setting and general social work practice. The requirements for the qualification state that you must experience at least two different service user groups during your practice learning plus statutory experience:

➢ http://www.dh.gov.uk/en/
Publicationsandstatistics/
Publications/
PublicationsPolicyAndGuidance/
DH_4007803 *page 3, Section J.*

The guide is primarily for social work students in the United Kingdom, though there are considerable parallels with placements for other students in health, social care and education.

There are increasing differences in the requirements for students in the four countries of the UK. Where these are significant, the differences will be mentioned or explored.

⊡1 the Laming Report 2009: http://publications.everychildmatters.gov.uk/eOrderingDownload/HC-330.pdf

TROUBLE

The vast majority of placements are enjoyable, even life-changing experiences. Placements are remembered in a way that class-based experiences tend not to be. For students this is usually a time of growth, not always without some pain, but usually significant. For supervisors it is an exciting chance to help to develop someone's professional identity and also to reflect on your own practice and expose it to an audience.

Not all placements go well. However, this is not inevitable; there is usually a chain of events that leads to the breakdown of a placement, so there is always the possibility of breaking this chain.

We hope that the advice in this guide will help you to be an active participant in the placement, not one who feels that events are controlling you. In *The Going Gets Tough* (▷147) you can find out more about what can go wrong, how you might anticipate this, and what you might do to prevent, confront or avoid it.

Most important is to understand what you can do if you begin to experience the placement going awry – whether as student, supervisor or tutor – and to discuss this possibility from the very start. Although there is a superstition that discussing something causes it to happen, the truth is actually the contrary – talking about the possibility decreases chances of it happening.

The seeds for success or failure are sown in the preparation for the placement and the way in which the arriving is handled (▷*Student role* 47). Open communication from the very first contact is the key to a successful outcome.

FELLOW TRAVELLERS

In your travels through this guide you will meet other people who are also taking journeys through social work education. Their experiences will provide a regular backdrop, giving you different perspectives on placements. Here we briefly introduce you to twelve of them. You will get to know them better during your journey.

STUDENTS

Shama Bindana is a South Asian woman in her late twenties. Shama is a teacher but has decided that she wants to retrain as a social worker. With family responsibilities, Shama works in residential care and is studying part-time at a local urban university. Following a car accident in her late teens, Shama uses a wheelchair.

Nat Davies is a 24-year-old white man who graduated in philosophy, politics and economics, and worked for six months on a community project in Chad before returning to England where he is a student on a two-year Masters social work programme in a rural area.

Mary O'Connor is an 18-year-old woman from an Irish Catholic family. She is a student on a three-year social work degree programme in a suburban university. She has some experience of volunteering with young people with learning disabilities and she has an older brother with Down's syndrome.

Brenda Shapiro is a white woman in her forties who has worked in social care many years. She started as a social work assistant in a generic social services department, then moved to adult services working with older people in a rural county. She is studying part time with a distance-learning programme.

Tara Watson is a 22-year-old African-Caribbean woman

studying full-time on a three-year social work degree programme in a large city. She missed some schooling, but returned to study in her late teens. She is the eldest in a large family.

SUPERVISORS

Dave Murray is an African-Caribbean social worker who completed the Practice Teaching Award some years ago and is an experienced supervisor. He works in statutory mental health services and he provides off-site support to students as well as supervising one-to-one. Currently he is acting team leader.

Cheryl Stone is a work-based supervisor in a community-based children and families agency. She is not qualified in social work. Cheryl has undertaken a three-day course in practice education and is about to supervise her first student from a social work course.

SERVICE USERS

Susan Chapman is a white service user who manages her own budget. She uses a wheelchair and she is part of a new project to see whether people who manage their own budgets might offer placements to social work students.

John Patterson is a 43-year-old black man who uses social services. He is a member of the service user and carers forum, which provides a variety of services for the local social work degree programme, including involvement in selection of students, assessment and teaching on the course. He is also a member of a community group that provides placements and a member of the Practice Assessment Panel (▷143).

TUTORS

Ali Chowdrey is a South Asian senior lecturer on two-year masters and three-year undergraduate social work programmes. He tutors eight to ten students in each year and provides the placement support from the university for these students.

Sandra Townsend is the Director of Practice Studies for a three-year degree programme in social work. In addition to providing tutorial support for two or three students each year, she coordinates the practice education for all the students on the course.

MANAGER

Viv Delaney is the Practice Development Manager for a large county. She leads a small team of practice development workers who are charged with coordinating and developing practice education in the local authority and with other agencies and organisations able to offer social work placements.

USING THE GUIDE

The guide is designed to help social work students get the best from their placements. It also aims to assist supervisors (the collective term for work-based supervisors, practice teachers, mentors and practice assessors), tutors and those with strategic responsibility for practice learning.

The research for the guide draws on formal studies and informal practice experience, in the hope that, together, these will create an accurate and engaging map of the placement.

The guide's reference point is the social work landscape, but there are many points of contact with other professions' practice learning. This is increasingly so as students from different professions find themselves learning in the same services and organisations.

The guide uses a travel guide format, in the belief that a placement has much in common with visiting a new place and that practice learning can be understood as a kind of journey. Along the way you will hear from fellow travellers whose backgrounds were briefly presented above. They will tell their stories in blogs (💬) punctuating the text.

Each chapter stands alone, with cross-references to related themes Even so, the guide does benefit from a full reading, so you have an idea of the entire landscape before setting foot in it. Also, follow up the website links (▷**W**) where you will find examples of various placement documents.

Above all, the guide hopes to prepare and sustain you and to be an encouragement for you to get the very best out of the valuable experience that is a placement.

PART TWO

THE

GUIDE

CHAPTER ONE

DOCUMENTATION

J ust as travellers must make sure they have the right paperwork – passport, visa, tickets, currency – so you need to get to grips with placement documentation to have a successful trip. The documentation can be complex, so it is important that everybody involved in the placement is aware of what its purposes are and how it is used. There should be regular opportunities for those with responsibility for the *protocols* for the placement to review whether these are supporting the placements in the way intended, so changes can be made in consultation with those who use them regularly. The documentation associated with a placement can seem bureaucratic and burdensome, but if it is well designed it will provide a strong framework to understand what the placement is about and for collecting the evidence of learning and practice competence that is required.

Links

Background information about *Fellow travellers* ▷09–11.
More explanation of terms ▷*Language* 226–8.
The following topics have strong links with themes in this chapter: *Codes of practice* ▷52; *Placement protocols for tough going* ▷163.
Examples of placement documents are indicated by ▷**W**, and can be downloaded at: www.routledge.com/textbooks/9780415499125.

Preliminaries

The documentation needed to arrive successfully at the placement (never mind complete it) can make you feel that you are entering a maze. To make it more manageable, consult the *Course Handbook* – and the *Placement Handbook* if this is a separate document – so that you know it inside out. There will be a list of the documents that you will need before and during the placement (if not, ask for one). Make yourself a checklist and gather together the essential documentation you will need before arriving at the placement, ticking each one off as you successfully complete it.

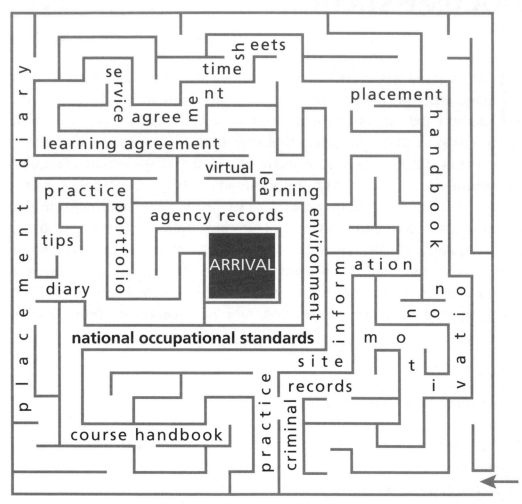

✦   *Chart 1.1: Placement maze*

📁 Criminal records

We noted in The Basics that you will need to complete a *Criminal Records Bureau* check (CRB) (▷03). The social work programme will inform you when and how this check must be completed – in addition to the check that the General Social Care Council (GSCC) registration will require. If you have a criminal record it is natural to be concerned about the consequences of this. The most important consideration is whether you have disclosed this at an early stage and discussed it with the programme's admissions tutor. The nature of your criminal activity, the circumstances surrounding it and how recently it occurred are all important factors that the programme will consider, as well as your own response to these events and your openness with the programme.

CRIMINAL RECORD BUREAU CHECKS

I organise the Criminal Record Bureau checks for the social work programme and I'd say we have about 10% of our students with a record of some sort. My own view is that these kinds of experience can actually have a positive side for the student, but it all depends how they've handled it since the conviction. Occasionally they deny it even when the conviction turns up; they've convinced themselves that it didn't actually get as far as that. I have quite a redemptive view of social work, but it's not always shared by the agencies (a few do their own checks in addition to ours) and what I try to emphasise to students is that it's no good me being very liberal now if down the line no agency will give them a placement. No placement, no qualification.

Sandra Townsend, director of practice studies

DOOR 1   THE RECKONING   DOOR 2

I was cautioned for shoplifting two years ago when I was 16. It was wrong, I knew it at the time – there were reasons, but they don't excuse it. I was very worried that it might mean I couldn't do the social work course so I phoned the admissions tutor at the time I was writing the application. My first thought was not to mention it on the form, to get an interview so they could see what I was like, then to let them know once they'd had a chance to hear me out. When I spoke with the admissions tutor, they explained the policy (it has to be two years ago which, thankfully it was – just). They wanted a character reference to show that I had learned from the experience and that I had changed. I'm so glad I confronted it.

Mary O'Connor, student

I'd put it completely to the back of my mind. 'Mary then' and me now were completely different people – there were very good reasons why she did what she did then, and good reasons why I would never contemplate doing that now. Now I am 18, legally an adult, and I knew everyone would see what potential I had to make a really good social worker.

When it came through positive, I suppose I knew this day was going to come but I'd put it out of my mind so completely I hadn't even rehearsed what I was going to say when they called me in. It was all like a bad dream, sort of slow motion. They said it was less about the crime and more about my 'integrity' – not declaring on the forms. I had to leave the course.

Mary O'Connor, student

You need to be aware that responses can vary from programme to programme and it is really important to check your position *at the point of application* (🕮1).

🗁 Course and placement handbooks

It may not be bedtime reading, but it is essential to get to know the *Handbook* thoroughly. The information about placements might be incorporated into the general course handbook, but is more likely to be separate. Have a highlighter to hand when you read it so you can note those parts that are particularly important and to remind you of any questions you want to ask. Find out who you should approach with questions – your tutor, the year tutor, the placement coordinator, the module leader for practice learning? Make sure your question is not already answered in the *Handbook* or on the course electronic sharepoint site – if 20 people ask the same question, and it is one that is already answered in the *Handbook*, the most saintly tutor is entitled to become irritable.

If you are offering a placement, you also need a copy of the *Handbook*. Some social work programmes have one handbook for all, others will have a placement handbook tailored for people providing placements. Increasingly, this is likely to be electronic, but if you require a different format ask for one. The placement handbook usually contains copies of the *protocols* that will be used for the placement.

📁 National Occupational Standards

There is general guidance and governance of the social work degree at national level (⊠1). Day-to-day direction for the student's practice education in England is guided by the National Occupational Standards (NOS) for social work (⊠2).

There are six *key roles*, each of which include a number of *units*. Each unit is spelled out further, with a number of *elements* and *performance criteria*; the standards are also likely to be included in your programme's *Course Handbook*. Below is a summary of the six key roles and the 21 units.

Key Role 1
  Prepare for, and work with individuals, families, carers, groups and communities to assess their needs and circumstances
Unit 1 Prepare for social work contact and involvement
Unit 2 Work with individuals, families, carers, groups and communities to help them make informed decisions
Unit 3 Assess needs and options to recommend a course of action

Key Role 2

Plan, carry out, review and evaluate social work practice with individuals, families, carers, groups, communities and other professionals

Unit 4 Respond to crisis situations

Unit 5 Interact with individuals, families, carers, groups and communities to achieve change and development and to improve life opportunities.

Unit 6 Prepare, produce, implement and evaluate plans with individuals, families, carers, groups, communities and professional colleagues

Unit 7 Support the development of networks to meet assessed needs and planned outcomes

Unit 8 Work with groups to promote growth, development and independence

Unit 9 Address behaviour which presents a risk to individuals, families, carers, groups and communities

Key Role 3

Support individuals to represent their needs, views and circumstances

Unit 10 Advocate with, and on behalf of, individuals, families, carers, groups and communities

Unit 11 Prepare for, and participate in decision making forums

Key Role 4

Manage risk to individuals, families, carers, groups, communities, self and colleagues

Unit 12 Assess and manage risks to individuals, families, carers, groups and communities

Unit 13 Assess, minimise and manage risk to self and colleagues

Key Role 5

Manage and be accountable, with supervision and support, for your own social work practice within your organisation

Unit 14 Manage and be accountable for your own work

Unit 15 Contribute to the management of resources and services

Unit 16 Manage, present and share records and reports

Unit 17 Work within multi-disciplinary and multi-organisational teams, networks and systems

Key Role 6

   Demonstrate professional competence in social work practice

*Unit 18 Research, analyse, evaluate, and use current knowledge of best
       social work practice*

*Unit 19 Work within agreed standards of social work practice and ensure
       own professional development*

Unit 20 Manage complex ethical issues, dilemmas and conflicts

Unit 21 Contribute to the promotion of best social work practice

SUSAN AND THE OCCUPATIONAL STANDARDS

As a service user who manages my own budget and with no social work training I was concerned about whether I could offer a placement to a social work student that would meet the student's needs. However, the programme gave us some training to prepare us (and the students) for this 'non-traditional' placement. We were introduced to the occupational standards. It was a bit much to take in to begin with, but we learned that students would only have to meet some of the standards in the time they were on placement with us. I mapped out Unit 7, to show what I thought this would mean for a student on a placement with me.

Unit 7 Support the development of networks to meet assessed needs and planned outcomes

In this Unit you will be expected to demonstrate your ability to:

- Examine with individuals, families, carers, groups, communities and others, support networks which can be accessed and developed.

- Work with individuals, families, carers, groups, communities and others to initiate and sustain support networks.

- Contribute to the development and evaluation of support networks.

1. Identify the different statutory/voluntary organisations that support the individual you are working with.

2. Reflect on the outcomes to be achieved and who might contribute what to the process.

3. Reflect on the way that people from the named organisations work together or where there are potential areas of conflict.

4. Are the intended outcomes achieved or not? Reflect on your role in working with the individual and how you might support him/her to achieve independent living outcomes.

Complete a life history of the person you are on placement with.
Listening, collaboration, presentation

Map the outcomes against people involved in their achievement, identifying and making explicit particular contributions.
Processing and ordering information

Meet with some of the workers involved and summarise potential useful collaboration and potential areas of conflict in their organisational policies.
Selection of specific information, communication

A personal statement about which outcomes are achieved and how you could contribute to improvement.
Reflection, interpretation, identification

Susan Chapman, service user provider
with acknowledgments to Christine Barton, service user placement provider

There are indications from research findings that the National Occupational Standards help supervisors who are not qualified as social workers to understand what social work is (◳3), as is illustrated by Susan Chapman's story (▷*Susan and the occupational standards*, 22). However, we will see later that this competence based approach is not without its critics, some of whom see it as being at odds with the development of more critical thinking, referred to as 'reflective practice' (▷*Reflection* 73; ▷*Competence and reflection*, 97; ▷*Competence*, 129).

🗁 Practice site information

☂ TOUR: WELCOME TO *FAMILY LINKS*

Family Links is a private organisation. The people who use our services are generally referred to us by social services and we work across a number of local authorities. We offer placements to two students at any one time.

What kinds of work will you get involved in?

You will work with children and families who are estranged from one another. We have both short and long-term involvement with families. You will experience a wide range of work – practical help, counselling, groupwork and project work. Either directly at *Family Links* or in collaboration with the local services, you will be able to meet all of the national occupational standards in this placement.

Who else will you work with?

As well as a team of five family support workers and two support staff on site, *Family Links* has good connections with social workers in the statutory agencies and we liaise closely with other professionals, such as healthcare workers, psychologists, schools and family law services.

How will you be supervised?

Family Links is new to social work placements – new and enthusiastic! You will have day-to-day supervision from a work-based supervisor and fortnightly sessions with an off-site practice teacher, who will see you individually and also in a group of six students all on placement locally.

Cheryl Stone, work-based supervisor

Placement finding is a mix of formal and informal networks (▷*Arriving*, 38). Increasingly, there is an expectation that those who offer placements should provide brief and accessible information about what they can offer in the style of a brochure. This gives students and tutors a flavour of what kind of work the site does, and so what kinds of opportunity for learning are available. It should also be honest about what opportunities might *not* be available; for example, there may be some National Occupational Standards that it would not be possible to achieve at a particular practice site, but this might not be problematic if the site is part of a larger placement package (▷*Multi-site placements*, 186). The placement information might also be available at the site's website or on a DVD, and it could be presented as a video.

📁 Learning Agreement

Early in the social work training programme is the time to talk about learning goals and preferences for placements. This same process will be repeated before each placement (usually two and sometimes three in each programme) and a pro-forma will be used to record the outcomes of these discussions. These pro-formas are usually sent to those who provide placements, as part of the process of deciding where students will go. Of course, the number and range of placements are limited so it is important to take a 'reality check' rather than have very fixed ideas about where the placement should be.

▷**W** for an example of a completed *Learning Agreement*.

MOTIVATION

My brother has Down's and the experience of growing up with him has given me a special awareness and commitment to learning disability. I know that's what I'll want to do when I qualify – it's been a lifelong ambition of mine. I know about the requirement to work with two different client groups and I'm feeling a bit anxious about this.

Mary O'Connor, student

THE BROADER PERSPECTIVE

A student's reason for choosing social work might stem from a very particular experience or motivation. I respect Mary O'Connor's personal experiences and the commitment this has given her. My responsibility as her tutor is to build on her motivation, helping her to widen her horizons. The degree and the professional qualification that goes with it is in *social work*; as such, it is broader than any particular client group. I hope the course will encourage Mary to be open to learning about social work practice in general, and not to see it as a specific training in working with learning disability.

It's common for students to be anxious about the placement, especially if it's going to be in a setting that's completely new to them. It helps if I know the setting, but that's not always the case. Good preparation is the key, though you can't prepare for everything and you just hope the student can also take some initiative.

Our first-year students have a session with some of the third years, who are generally quite reasonable and realistic about their experiences; it's good for the first-year students to see how they are likely to grow over the course of their studies.

Ali Chowdrey, tutor.

Any other considerations

As well as considering individual learning goals, the Learning Agreement is an opportunity to consider any other needs. Reasonable requests are treated sympathetically, for example when personal circumstances make distant travel difficult – but no guarantees can be given about the location of placements and there is need for compromise.

In addition to the your individual learning needs as a student, the Learning Agreement will record the specific opportunities available at the site of the placement and how these match (or don't) your learning needs. It is an Agreement, not a statement, so there can be some brokering between your needs and what the practice site can offer; when you add these together, this becomes 'The Placement'. As stated earlier, the National Occupational Standards can help translate the working practices at the site into the specific social work standards that must be achieved.

It is not tempting fate to discuss what would happen if things started to go wrong in the placement. Establishing these ground rules will help put in place mechanisms to avoid difficulties, but if they do occur having the protocols (such as informal and formal arrangements and complaints procedures) named in the Learning Agreement will help everyone (▷*Protocols for placement breakdown*, 163).

FERRY TO THE PLACEMENT

Despite all the changes over the years there are some things that are pretty much the same – not wanting to travel to placements is one of them! I wasn't too happy about my first placement when I trained back in the 1970s – it entailed a drive to a ferry, a ferry across a river, a train ride to the town, then bus journeys to see the clients – all in the winter months. The placement was two and a half days a week, so as a trade-off for the long, tortuous journey, two longer days were permitted to save me having to do the journey three times a week. It wasn't easy, but it turned out to be a great placement.

Viv Delaney, practice development manager

Insurance

Your Learning Agreement will also include details of insurance arrangements. First, as a student you will need car-for-business-use insurance if you intend using your car for work. As a placement provider you should check that your third party insurance will cover the student.

🗁 Service Agreement

Who is party to the Learning Agreement? The inner circle in Chart 1.2 represents the Learning Agreement, with the student at its centre. The tutor is likely to be the broker for the agreement, and this will certainly involve the on-site person who will be providing the hands-on everyday work with you. Sometimes this will be a qualified social worker with practice teaching experience and training (often called a *singleton practice teacher*), in which case it might not be necessary to involve any other person directly in the Learning Agreement. However, if this is a *work-based supervisor* without a social work qualification and little or no experience of practice education, then it will be necessary to involve an *off-site supervisor*, qualified in social work and experienced in practice teaching. This person will provide the opportunity for you to reflect on your experiences at the site through the specific prism of social work. This might be individually, in groups, or both (▷*Group supervision*, 112).

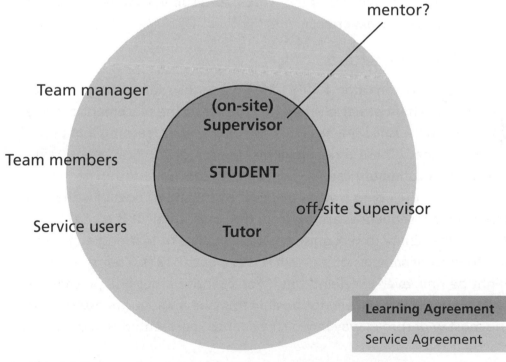

+ *Chart 1.2: Learning Agreement and Service Agreement*

The Learning Agreement lies at the heart of a broader *Service Agreement* (different from a service level agreement between the social work programme and the practice agencies) about the service that you can expect from the placement: who will provide what; to whom will you have access, and with what frequency? As the outer circle indicates, there are other people with a stake in the placement: the rest of the team at the placement site, the manager of that team and the people who use the service. These people may not be directly involved in brokering the Learning Agreement, but they will be playing a part in the Service Agreement.

In addition, a work-based supervisor might have access to a mentor to help them with the role; the mentoring might be provided by someone separate from the practice site or perhaps by the team manager. The mentor is not in direct contact with the student and therefore is unlikely to figure in the Agreement; even so, the availability of a mentor might influence the effectiveness of the work-based supervision which, as the student, you would experience directly.

🗁 Practice portfolio

The placement is an opportunity to learn about social work in practice and a place where practice is taught. The site of the placement provides direct experiences for practice. It is also where your learning and practice will be assessed. These three elements – learning, practice, assessment – must be documented carefully. Indeed, the documentation of the learning and the doing is what makes the assessment possible. There are important consequences arising from this: most of all, it is crucial to develop the ability to recognise what is evidence of learning and practice, and to present samples of it (▷*What is evidence?* 125). Your practice might be fine, even excellent, but if you cannot gather and present the evidence for it, others will not be able to make an accurate assessment. The most widespread way in which evidence is presented is in a portfolio.

The term *portfolio* is used commonly but in fact portfolios can vary widely – there is a huge variation in what the term means in practice. It originates from the notion of the artists' portfolios, which contain examples of their work – landscape, portrait, abstract, oil, water, charcoal and, these days, probably video examples of art installations. Portfolios let the viewer actually see a sample of the range and quality of the artists' work – direct evidence of their practical and conceptual abilities. A social work portfolio is more difficult because professional practice is as much a process as it is a product, and it is 'four-dimensional' – an interactive process over time that is not easily captured in the two dimensions of a portfolio. Nevertheless, the original portfolios were designed to capture a broad range of social work activities via audio- and videotapes and flipchart inclusions, not just conventional prose ($\triangleright$ *Brief History*, 224).

So, you need to get to know the protocols for your portfolio – how it is structured and what kinds of evidence you are expected to present. Think of it this way: it is hard to give a good performance as a pianist if your piano is not well tuned. So, if you don't get attuned to your portfolio documentation, you will fail to give the best presentation of your work.

SURVIVAL OF THE FITTEST

As the Practice Development Manager for a large county, I work with a number of different social work programmes. We've tried to harmonise the assessment systems in this region because supervisors don't like working with a whole load of different portfolios – it's hard for small voluntary organisations, too, they just don't have the infrastructure to handle masses of paperwork. It's not that we want the portfolio to be easy for students, but it can be demanding without being confusing and over-complex. It's nice when they use plain English. One programme had massive lists of competences with cross-referencing and all sorts; in the end some of the placements just said, don't send us students from that course, send them from the other – and it was purely on account of the portfolio system. They could get to grips with one and found the other cumbersome and very time-consuming. It's a question of survival of the fittest – fittest for purpose!

Viv Delaney, practice development manager

Frequently, a portfolio will require you to present evidence in terms of *descriptions* of your practice (what happened), *analyses* of the practice (how and why it happened), and *reflections* on both the practice and learning (what you think of it now and how you might do things differently with your fresh understandings). There is usually a requirement to link this to theoretical frameworks. The evidence will also need to be tied to the learning objectives which have been detailed in your Learning Agreement, and to some or all of the National Occupational Standards.

The first encounter with a portfolio is usually daunting, but it begins to make more sense as you start to use it. Access to good examples of completed portfolios is helpful so you can see how others have worked with the portfolio (📚2/ **W**). Supervisors also need to make themselves familiar with the portfolio structure so they can help the student, especially in the initial stages of recognising what is evidence. You should also document your own *teaching*, whether for formal evidence (if undertaking continuing education, such as Enabling Learning modules in England or the Scottish Practice Learning qualifications) or just for your own record of development.
(▷**W** for an example of a completed placement portfolio.)

✎ Portfolio tips

Check first with the specific guidelines that your social work course provides. What follows are general tips for students compiling their portfolios.

- ✎ Get organised. This means organising your thinking so you are familiar with the structure of the portfolio. It means organising a folder so when you jot down examples of learning and practice you know roughly where to put them. This helps when you come to edit your portfolio later.
- ✎ Read a completed portfolio. Ask for examples of successful portfolios to give you an idea of what they look like.
- ✎ Check you know what 'evidence' means. Discuss hypothetical examples of evidence so you feel confident about gathering the real stuff.

- ✗ Act quickly. Jot down examples from your learning and practice soon after they happen. You'll forget them if you don't. You can go back to them at a later date to fill in the details.
- ✗ Get support. If you have problems with writing don't try to hide it; make sure you get the support you need *before* you start your placement. Work on your computer skills if these are holding you back.
- ✗ Learn from your mistakes. Your portfolio is where you demonstrate your *learning* as well as your practical skills. Use the portfolio to show how you handled a situation that didn't go to plan, and reflect on what differences your learning has made to your practice during the placement.
- ✗ Include the service user's voice. Check what the programme has to say about including feedback from service users in your portfolio. Think about how you are going to incorporate the service user's voice meaningfully and fairly.
- ✗ Select widely. Your portfolio can only be a *sample* of your placement experience – it is impossible to record and reflect on everything. So check that you have examples of different kinds of activity and experience.
- ✗ Keep your Learning Agreement to hand. Have a regular check (during supervision?) that the learning objectives are being met and that the evidence you are gathering matches them. Check you are meeting the required National Occupational Standards.
- ✗ Link practice and theory and do some reading, if only the notes that you made in lectures. The portfolio is not just a description of what you did, it needs to be analysed, reflected on and related to your understanding of relevant theory (▷*Mapping*, 78).
- ✗ Make your values explicit. 'Values' can seem woolly and abstract, so your portolio is a chance to make them real and concrete. Start by using hypothetical examples with your supervisor, so you get used to talking about the values that underpin your practice (▷*Testing values*, 136).
- ✗ Edit and proofread. The quality of work is reflected in the quality of your portfolio, rightly or wrongly, so make sure you read through the finished work and make whatever corrections are needed.
- ✗ Finally, don't think assessment is like an exam – that it all comes at the end of the learning. Start building your portfolio from Day One and

make sure you do some writing for it every week at the very least –
you should be making brief notes pretty much every day. So, don't
leave it all to the last minute.

Other Documentation

As well as specific placement documentation, there is other
documentation that students and others connected to the placement will
need to manage.

🗁 Agency records

LEARNING TO RECORD AND LEARNING *ABOUT* RECORDING

I was recently invited to talk to a group of new supervisors who were
on a three-day course to support their practice teaching. I offered
this insight.

A light bulb came on for me when I realised that my job as a
supervisor was not so much to teach the student how to fill in the
forms in *my* agency, but more generally how to understand the
purpose of recording in general. Yes, they need to be able to handle
the systems in my particular workplace, and to complete a
reasonably competent assessment – though they are students, so
they'll make more mistakes than most. But it's my business to help
them understand the principles that underpin the practices, so they
know *why* this is a good piece of recording; that way, they will know
how to work with the protocols of other agencies even when they
are very different ones. And to work with them critically.

I remind students that, though we have to use a formal assessment
document with our service users, the *social work* behind it is essentially
to help people to tell their stories. The assessment form, whatever
shape it takes, is just a way of helping to gather people's stories in a
systematic way. That way, the students start with the *person* and not
with the form and they'll take that knowledge and competence with
them, to whatever setting they are placed in or work in.

Dave Murray, supervisor

In addition to all the paperwork associated with the placement, the practice site has its own systems for recording, its own *agency protocols*. These vary from site to site, from the relatively informal to the relatively formal. It is important for you to learn about these protocols and to differentiate between documentation for the purposes of your *placement* and recording for the purposes of the *practice site*. Sometimes agency recording can be included in the placement documentation, but it must be clearly anonymised, with identifying details removed (not just names but anything else that might identify the service users). Your ability to work with the practice site's recording protocols is part of your assessment.

🗀 Placement diary

It probably feels like you have enough to document without taking time out to reflect on all of this in a diary or log. Even so, this kind of *reflective log* is a real bonus to help you look back over the course of your learning – a series of snapshots that, taken together, show your growth during the placement (⌂4). Some courses make this a requirement so that your log is part of the formal placement documentation, but even if it is not a must, it is certainly to be recommended.

A placement diary is also very helpful if things start to go wrong. Whether student or supervisor, having your own personal account of developments during the placement will help to put it into perspective and perhaps provide an *audit trail* of how things got to where they did. The placement diary should not be an alternative to talking about difficulties with the people concerned, but it can be a good way of rehearsing what you might want to say and how (▷*Defusing placement time-bombs* 158. ▷**W** for an example of an entry in a placement diary).

🗀 Service user and colleague feedback

The guide looks in more detail at service user feedback in Chapter 10, but it is vital at the very beginning of the placement to consider how this will be gathered fairly and sensitively. Many programmes and agencies have their own pro-formas and, though these can provide a helpful framework, you need to think how feedback from service users can be more meaningful than tick-boxes or a brief questionnaire. For example, are there methods of social work practice where feedback is integral to the work itself, so that it is not an 'add-on'? (☜3). Finding out from service users how they are experiencing your work is good practice as well as useful evidence for your portfolio (▷*Service user feedback*, 212).

Other members of the team and other professionals who have experienced your work can have valuable insights on your practice; they may have seen you in quite different circumstances from your supervisor, for example. It is rather too easy to be very casual about gathering colleague feedback, and a hearsay approach should be avoided. Likely colleagues should be identified well before the end of the placement and the format of the feedback (a short questionnaire, a written testimony, etc) should be agreed beforehand. It is important to find ways in which support staff – such as reception and secretarial colleagues and interpreters, where they have been needed – can provide feedback, too. Where a colleague might wish to make critical feedback it is important that this is properly evidenced and that the student has an opportunity to comment on the feedback within the final documentation.
(▷**W** for an example of service user feedback.)

🗀 Time sheets, payment schedules, etc

Check with the training programme what other documentation is necessary. For example, there is likely to be a time sheet to be completed to make sure you complete the correct number of days. You must complete a minimum of 200 days of practice learning during the course of the programme. There will need to be a record of any absences, with reasons. Make sure you are aware of the options available to you if these requirements are not met (▷*Possible outcomes* 167).

Agencies claiming the daily placement fee for the student should enquire before the placement starts about the invoicing system and how and when payments are made (▷*Currency*, 05).

OTHER LIKELY DOCUMENTS

> ➤ Checklist/Flowchart for placement documentation ▷**W**
> ➤ Health and safety policy
> ➤ Codes of practice
> ➤ Placement monitoring ▷208
> ➤ Placement evaluation forms ▷208
> ➤ Feedback forms ▷212
> ➤ Supervision notes ▷116

Virtual Learning Environments

Increasingly, social work courses are using *virtual learning environments* (VLEs) such as Blackboard, Moodle and Wimba for students to keep in touch with tutors and/or other students between class contacts. Lectures, powerpoints, handouts and assignments are likely to be posted on these sites, with students entering through a password-protected *portal*. The placement documentation and other protocols for the course are also likely to be kept on the VLE site (▷*The virtual placement*, 60; ▷*Social networking*, 74).

◰ Click to download

◰1 Requirements for Social Work Training
England ▷ www.dh.gov.uk
Relevant documents for England ▷ http://www.dh.gov.uk/en/Publicationsandstatistics/Publications/PublicationsPolicyAndGuidance/DH_4007803
Northern Ireland ▷ www.niscc.info
Relevant documents for Northern Ireland
▷ www.niscc.info/NISCC_Standards_Honours_Degree_Social_Work-80.aspx
Scotland ▷ www.sssc.uk.com
The Framework for social work education in Scotland
▷ www.sssc.uk.com/preparingforpractice/pdf/siswe.pdf
Wales ▷ www.ccwales.org.uk

⊡2 The National Occupational Standards for social work:
   ▷ www.skillsforcare.org.uk

⊡3 These two research reports identify the significance of the National
   Occupational Standards, especially for non-social work sites:
   ▷ Doel, M., Nelson, P., Flynn, E. and Mulrooney, C. (2008), *How
     New Projects and Initiatives in Social Work Practice Learning
     Successfully Mature*, Leeds: Skills for Care and CWDC
     www.skillsforcare.org.uk
   ▷ Doel, M., Nelson, P., Flynn, E. and Mulrooney, C. (2009), *Sustaining
     Practice Learning with Local Authorities*, Leeds: Skills for Care/
     CWDC www.skillsforcare.org.uk

⊡4 An example of a reflective blog, this one about travel:
   ▷ http://inindia09.blogspot.com/

⊡5 A report on the development of e-portfolios in nursing and business:
   Duffy, K., Anthony, D. and Vickers, F. (2008), 'Are e-portfolios an
   asset to learning and placement?' ASET, De Montford University
   ▷ www.asetonline.org

📖 Books, articles, research reports

📚1 This article discusses the issues surrounding decisions about criminal
   convictions and entry into social work education:
   ▷ Cowburn, M. and Nelson, P. (2008), 'Safe recruitment, social
     justice, and ethical practice: should people who have criminal
     convictions be allowed to train as social workers?' *Social Work
     Education*, 27:3 pp293–306.

📚2 An example of a completed portfolio has been published in:
   Doel, M., Sawdon, C. and Morrison, D. (2002), *Learning, Practice and
   Assessment*, London: Jessica Kingsley.
   The portfolio (Part Two of the book) demonstrates how a social
   worker gathered her evidence of learning and practice of
   groupwork.

📚3 A social work practice method which has service user feedback built in:
   ▷ Marsh, P. and Doel, M. (2005), *The Task-Centred Book*, London:
     Routledge/Community Care.

CHAPTER TWO

ARRIVING

F irst impressions can be very important. Unless it has been a very last-minute affair, you will have had some contact with the placement before you start, perhaps even a formal interview. The first few days are significant ones that will set the tone for the rest of the placement. This is true both of the impression that you make as a student and the impression that the practice site makes as a placement. For students who are also practitioners the challenge is how to make this seem like a true *arrival*, not merely a return. This chapter considers the nature of the student role – the similarities and the differences between a student in the placement and an employee in the agency. Ground rules need agreeing early on in order to help each party to understand their expectations and responsibilities and to negotiate any differences that emerge. Placements on more than one site and placements which involve more than one student are also considered.

Links

Background information about your *Fellow travellers* ▷09–11.
More explanation of terms in *Language* ▷226–8.
The following topics have strong links with the themes in this chapter:
Practice curriculum ▷80; *Pre-test* ▷121; *From placement to placement* ▷193; *Re-arrival* ▷199.
Examples of placement documents are indicated by ▷**W**, and can be downloaded at: www.routledge.com/textbooks/9780415499125.

Preliminaries

As a placement provider you will need to ensure that a student has the necessary resources to make a success of the placement – space, computer access and the like. What will you do to make them feel welcome on their first day? As a student, prepare yourself mentally, in terms of what you are hoping to learn from this placement, whilst also being open to some unexpected learning opportunities. Make sure you know how to get to the practice site!

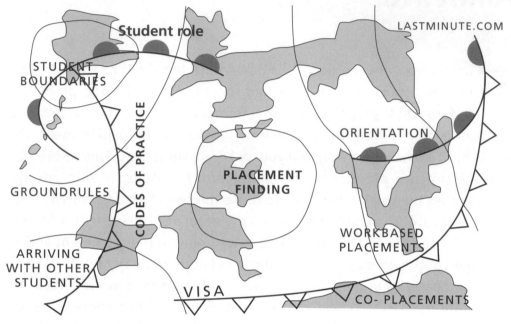

✦ *Chart 2.1: Always take the weather*

⚲ Placement finding

Social work courses are responsible for finding the placement, and first contact is nearly always between the course and the practice site (⌂1▷**W**); an exception is where your placement is also your work base, in which case you are already known (▷*When students are experienced practitioners*, 198). Each social work programme builds its bank of placements, in some cases developing long-standing relationships with the supervisors and, in larger organisations, with the persons who organise and coordinate placements, like Viv Delaney and her team (▷*A Placement Service*, below). In some cases there are formal arrangements, *service level agreements*, with local authorities, voluntary agencies and community groups. Some larger agencies have a formal policy that requires, or certainly expects, that each team or unit in the organisation will provide a placement for a specified number of students each year.

An increase in placement days from 120 in the previous diploma course to 200 in the current degree course, coupled with larger numbers of social work students, means greater demands on placement time. Programmes have responded by *creating* placements in addition to finding them. This active approach recognises that placements are not necessarily lying around to be discovered, but there are practice sites that have never considered offering a placement and these might be nurtured and developed so that they are in a position to do so. Some of these new placements are being found in traditional social work agencies, but also increasingly in 'non-traditional' areas. We will consider these in more detail in Chapter 8 (▷*Examples of placements off the beaten track*).

If you know of a possible placement, perhaps through a friend or relative, it is important to discuss it with your tutor or the director of practice studies on the course rather than make your own contact. It will be the course's responsibility to follow up and to decide whether the site is suitable to offer a placement, so do not feel tempted to 'scout' the site. Tip-offs such as this can be very valuable in discovering new placements, but it is vital that the formal processes are used to suss them out.

For students sponsored by your agency and expected to have a placement in your worksite the challenge is not the finding of the placement but the *transforming* of the worksite into a placement site. Placing students in their worksite is not without controversy, but if we unpick this, it concerns the perceived difficulties of transforming a workplace into a learning place. This is a general challenge: indeed, this is the core definition of a placement, *the transformation of workplace to learning place*. That is why the impact of a placement is so important for the team and the agency at large, because it has the potential to transform the practice agency into a learning organisation. The additional challenge for the student-worker is finding a way to transform your colleagues' perceptions of you from a practitioner to a learner (▷*Sponsored students* 199).

A PLACEMENT SERVICE

We followed the research into what makes for effective placements very carefully (⊠1,⊠2). We developed a strategy to embed practice learning throughout the authority. This meant changing job descriptions to make sure that qualified staff were expected to undertake supervision training and offer one placement a year. At the very least, each team is required to supervise at least one student each year. For our 'home-grown students' that we sponsor we have an arrangement with the neighbouring county to do a swap, so we take their sponsored students and they find placements for ours.

There was a wide consultation about the rewards that staff would value (again, this came strongly out of the research), resulting in quite a wide range of opinion. In the end it was decided that each team offering a placement would receive an honorarium – £500 that it could spend as it wanted (books and materials, training, team away-day, that kind of thing). Also, it was suggested that the Director should meet the students as a group at the end of their placement to see how they have found the experience. She does this regularly now and we often recruit this way! We have a monthly supervisors' forum which includes supervisors from some of the voluntary sector placements that we support.

We now have a service-led agreement with two of the local social work programmes. This helps their planning as well as ours because they know how many placements to expect from us and when. The programmes consult with us if any changes are mooted (student numbers, placement timing, assessment procedures, etc) so we can all plan in partnership. A third programme very much did its own thing and we no longer offer placements for them.

I see us as offering *a placement service*, not just individual placements.
Viv Delaney, practice development manager

So, the term 'placement finding' includes *placement maintenance* for existing sites that are used regularly, *placement creation* for new opportunities for practice learning, and *placement transformation* for worksites that will have to change into placements for existing practitioners who have taken a new role as students.

Remember that during the course of your social work training in England ◰3, you are required to have experience:

➢ in at least two practice settings
➢ of statutory social work tasks involving legal interventions
➢ of providing services to at least two user groups (e.g. child care and mental health).

Waiting for a placement can be a stressful time. It relies on a great deal of trust between students and tutors and a belief that all is being done to provide the best placements available. Rather like waiting at a railway station for a train, or an airport for a plane, it is not necessarily the delay itself which causes greatest grief but the quality of the information available about the delay. That is why it is important for programmes to keep information channels open, and with virtual learning environments there are many different ways of maintaining communication; but students, too, must contain their anxiety and not overwhelm the programme with too frequent demands for information.

⧖ Lastminute.com

Planning and preparation represent good practice, but for some placements there is a last-minute scramble. Increasingly, the demands on placement finding described earlier mean that some placements do not start on the appointed date and/or the lead-in period is very short or absent altogether. Does this disadvantage you as a student? Well, the guide will be making much reference to 'mindset' so you will not be surprised to read that much depends on the way you approach this last-minute experience. If you can develop the confidence to see the placement as an adventure you will be able to turn this 'pack a toothbrush' experience into a positive rather than a negative. Some students can do this because it is part of their natural style (▷*Journey styles*, 55); for those of you who like your journey planned to the last detail, how might you get the best from this <last-minute.com> deal?

Your view of this last-minute placement will be coloured by the immediate history: is it last minute because you happened to be towards the end of the queue of students, so it was just a happenstance (somebody has to be towards the end)? Or did you make stringent demands in terms of the location and type of placement, and it was not possible to match these successfully? Or perhaps an earlier placement opportunity fell through? Again, the many different reasons why this could have happened will colour your current thinking.

Take time to reflect on these last-minute circumstances. Once you have analysed the reasons why the placement is starting late or has been arranged at the last minute, you can begin to set the actual placement – the one you have been offered – in context. Perhaps most difficult is if the last-minute placement falls a long way from your declared wishes and you are having to cope with disappointment as well as late planning. This is a good opportunity to find out how you *do* cope with disappointment; there will be plenty of disappointments along the path of your professional work, so you could see this as practice and a chance to learn some strategies to manage it. One suggestion is to make a list of everything the new placement looks likely to offer you that you had not been expecting. Another is to list the aspects that you think are going to be difficult or disappointing (such as a long commute to the placement) and force yourself to turn each one into a positive (such as the extra time it will give for reflection or to catch up on your reading).

Most important of all is to find a way to share your thoughts and feelings with your supervisor in a way that is not complaining or rejecting (remember, this is the person who has offered you a placement, and they probably have feelings about it being last minute, too) and which looks honestly at the pros and cons of what has happened.

☿ 'Visa' for practice learning

It is important that you are prepared for practice learning even if you are not yet aware of your specific placement arrangements. A 'light touch' approach to testing your readiness for placement is designed to protect the people who use services and ensure that valuable placements will be put to good use. The *Readiness for Practice Learning* arrangements are rather like gaining your visa for the forthcoming placement.

VISA FOR A NEW STATE (OF MIND)

With over 15 years of experience in social care, and as a part-time student who's working the rest of the week in this field, I resented having to be tested for my 'readiness' and, not being one to keep my mouth shut, I said as much. I have to say, my tutor was very good. He listened to me and he was sympathetic, though now I think about it, he must have heard this same story many times before. He said to me: 'think of it as like applying for a visa to visit a new country.' I told him that's the point, it isn't a new country, but he said: 'but, you see, it is.' You're a student now – that's not to close our eyes to all your experience as a practitioner, but being a student is different to being a worker and the 'visa' is what shows the world that difference. And then it dawned on me and I said, yes, and I suppose it tells *me* that I'm a student, too. I suddenly saw myself very differently.

It's funny; when I got my transcript back (that's how they do the readiness thing on my course) I felt that it should have some kind of crest on it, like a visa would!

Brenda Shapiro, student

Each programme has designed its own methods to test your readiness, though each different protocol will have been approved by the General Social Care Council (GSCC) when the programme as a whole is validated.

For example, in one programme students spend 15 hours shadowing a social worker with at least 18 months' experience. The students then write a short piece (about 750 words) which considers their values in the light of their experiences during the shadowing. This piece is marked by an independent supervisor and, along with a report from the social worker whom the student shadowed, the whole is considered by a supervisor panel. The social worker bases their report on the GSCC Code of Practice (⊠4) which the student is expected to have read and signed. The system works so well that the programme has more social workers volunteering to be shadowed than it needs.

BETTER NOW THAN LATER

One student would have failed the Readiness for Practice Learning if we had had the right information at the time. It was only later that we heard from a supervisor that she was sad we hadn't taken up the comments she'd written – she'd taken the student with her for a visit and had asked the social worker who was collecting the information together to make a note of her concerns, but the social worker hadn't included them. The student was late for the interview, said she was hungry during the interview and ate a sandwich during the session, spoke of her own personal experience of domestic violence with the service user and subsequently mimicked the service user after the interview. This student's subsequent placement was terrible (including not turning up on time). We are now taking out a suitability case (▷166). Even the course student representative commented that other students were complaining that this student was being disruptive by regularly coming to lectures late.

Ali Chowdrey, tutor

Of course, a system works only if it is applied conscientiously, honestly and fairly. Sometimes people act in ways they think are kind, such as giving someone the benefit of the doubt, when in fact this merely defers a difficult decision. If you are not yet ready for practice or for practice learning it is better to know now rather than later, after you have put a lot of time into your studies. Tutor Ali Chowdrey's experience (opposite) is not unusual but it can be avoided if everyone involved in practice learning is open and honest from the outset. The student may have been spared the pain at the 'visa stage' but it is much more painful to be considered unsuitable at the later placement stage.

It is important to remind ourselves that these arrangements focus on the student's readiness for practice *learning*, not readiness for practice itself. It is not your practice that is being tested (how could it be at this stage?), but how ready you are to make use of the opportunity for a placement.

TOUR: STUDENT BOUNDARIES

There is much talk of the **student role**, but what is this? One way of determining how your role as a student differs from that of an employee or a member of the public is to consider the situations below, perhaps early in a supervision session.

Can you answer *Always* or *Never* to any of these 20 questions?

If your answer to a question is *It Depends*, what does it depend on?

OILING THE WHEELS

1 Will you refer to other staff at the placement as 'colleagues'?
2 Will you give your supervisor your mobile phone number?
 • will you expect to have your supervisor's mobile number?
 • their home phone number?
 • make a personal call from the practice site?
3 Would you ask for/accept practical help from your supervisor?
 • to advise you what's wrong with your car?
 • to mend an electrical fault?
4 Are there any circumstances in which you would have an alcoholic drink during the working day?
5 Would you talk about personal matters on placement?
6 Would you lend money to another worker in the agency?

SELF-DISCLOSURE

7 To which staff at the practice site would you talk about your work with service users?
8 Would you share personal information with others in the team?
 • good news, such as your partner being promoted?
 • bad news, like your father suffering from Alzheimer's?
9 Which, if any, of these badges might you expect to be able to wear on placement? Your supervisor?

Make up a slogan for the sixth badge. Would you comment if your supervisor wore any of the badges?
10 Would you expect to bring your child to the placement if your child-minding arrangements had failed?

SOCIAL CONTACT

11 Would you accept an invitation from a team member to:
 • her wedding?
 • his house-party?
 • an outing to the theatre?
12 In the evening, would you avoid a place you knew was frequented by your supervisor? Your tutor?

TOUCH

13 Do you expect to shake hands with your supervisor when you first meet?
14 Would you touch a member of the team who is upset?
 • on the arm?
 • round the shoulders?
 • on the knee?
15 Would you cuddle or play with your supervisor's children?

WHISTLE-BLOWING

Would you ignore or report:
16 ... a fellow student who claims to have a cannabis plant at home?
17 ... a team member who fiddles mileage claims?
18 ... a team member who fiddles mileage claims to pay for the expenses of a service user group?
19 ... a manager who has pornography in the desk drawer?
20 ... a team member who has written a false record?

Student role

The notion of role expectations, as a student, is not new to the placement setting and it might be helpful first to consider some dilemmas and boundary issues in relation to your role as a student in the academy. For example:

What would you do if ...

➤ A fellow student asked you to deliver their assignment for them
➤ A fellow student was disruptive by persistently coming to a lecture late
➤ You disagreed with the mark your assignment received
➤ Your assignment was not marked and returned within the specified period agreed by the programme
➤ A small group of students was disrespectful when you were doing a presentation in one of the seminar groups.

Your responses to these scenarios will give you an idea of how you are likely to see your role as a student when you move into the placement setting. It is likely that you will come to the placement as a relative unknown unless the placement is based where you are employed as a practitioner. The pre-placement visit and the *Learning agreement* (▷24), are all very important in helping to clarify the student role, but it is really when you are starting the placement that your role becomes something concrete and tangible. It is different from the student role in the class setting, and something akin to an apprentice, novice or trainee, though not actually any of these. *Learner* comes close as a description, but – like student – this term describes your role in class, so it does not convey the special flavour that comes from your position as a learner on placement.

Rather than discussing the student role in the abstract, one way of understanding what it might mean in practical terms is to take the *Student Boundaries* tour (▷46) together with the supervisor. The factors that could change your opinions or decisions are the interesting ones in terms of developing self-aware practice. You might throw even more light on the student role by discussing how your answers would alter if you were, say, an employee of the agency or a manager in the agency?

Another adaptation is to do Boundaries early on, making notes of your responses, and then to visit it again later in the placement to see how the two sets of responses compare and what might account for any differences.

Consider the two parallel lists below in which student and practitioner positions are contrasted. Make your own additions to this list, including possible similarities as well as differences, and reflect on the implications these contrasts have for the placement experience, not just for the student but for supervisors and their colleagues.

Student	Practitioner
learner	employee
temporary	permanent
orientation	induction
not paid	paid
not contracted to agency	contracted to agency
novice (but not always)	experienced
studying	practising
assessed	appraised
receives regular supervision	receives regular supervision?

✦ Orientation

It is usual to have a period of time very early in the placement, shortly after arrival, which introduces you to the practice site in a systematic way. This is often referred to as *induction*. However, the guide uses *orientation*, not just because this continues the analogy with the explorer or traveller, but because it differentiates your introduction to the placement from the induction that a new worker might receive as part of an introduction to a practice site. The new worker is, indeed, being inducted into the ways of working of the agency which now employs them; you, on the other hand, are being given an orientation to part of the social work landscape where you are a temporary visitor and where your role is not that of a new employee.

WHO'S DECAFFEINATED? 1

I was really excited by the coming placement – the placements were what I was most looking forward to – but I was quite nervous, too. I didn't really know what to expect and how I could get to know everything and everyone in such a short space of time. My supervisor had devised an orientation exercise that he gave me at our first session – he introduced it to me and checked I was OK with it. There were about 20 questions (previous students had made suggestions, too, and these had been included), all designed to get me out and about meeting people and finding things out. It worked well – people were primed, they knew I'd be coming to seek them out. There were some fun questions, too, like 'who takes their coffee decaffeinated?' It was an enjoyable way of getting to know people and systems quickly, but with a purpose.

Tara Watson, student

WHO'S DECAFFEINATED? 2

The 'Who's Decaffeinated?' exercise has built up over a few years now. At the end of the current student's placement I ask them to adapt it for the next student, which is a good way of making sure it keeps fresh and relevant – it's so hard to see a place as if for the first time when you've been here a long time. I tell the student it's a light-hearted introduction to the placement, which it is, but it's also a helpful informal insight to me of what this student is like. Are they likely to be able to take the initiative? Are they relatively flexible? How do they set about a task? Did they work through the questions in order or – if they didn't, how did they go about the exercise? This is all useful to understand how they tick. And it accelerates their entry into the placement.

Dave Murray, supervisor

The orientation should be organised so that it helps you to make sense of the new landscape of the placement. It is the first part of the mapping that we will continue to explore in Chapter 4. Orientation activities and exercises are one way of pointing you in directions that are important to your successful visit, whilst also being fun to do. There are many examples available now, though they all need to be tailored to the particular placement and, perhaps, to the specific student, too (⊠5).

Ground rules

When a new group begins it is very common to help the group develop a set of ground rules – expectations about the group, its behaviours and values. Similarly, in finding out what is expected of a student in a particular setting, and what you expect as a student, there should be an opportunity early on to discuss the ground rules. This need not be formalised (so it won't necessarily be part of the Learning Agreement), and it might be something that you would write about in your *Placement log* (▷33). A discussion of ground rules could be triggered first by completing the *Student boundaries* tour (▷46).

SOCIALWORKLAND BY CHAIR

It was a difficult call because obviously I wanted reassurance that the placement would not be an obstacle course for me as a wheelchair user, but I also wanted to experience the placement as any other student would. My supervisor was great. She had an orientation exercise that she used regularly, but she'd asked her previous (able-bodied) student to revisit it as if he used a wheelchair. It was a good exercise for him because he became more aware of disability issues, and it was a practical help for me because it threw up possible obstacles that my supervisor was able to sort out before I arrived. I enjoyed doing the exercise, too. The *Socialworkland* map in the guide was a good starting point – we looked at all the 'places' I would need to visit and, though it's not actually a physical place, nevertheless we took the idea further and considered what might be needed for a successful visit to *Socialworkland* by wheelchair. I found this very supportive and such a contrast to my second placement, more of which later …

Shama Bindana, student

Work-based placements

The student role is more complex when you are experiencing a placement on your home turf. If your placement is also your worksite, orientation to the *placement* as opposed to the practice site (which you already know well) is a tangible way of demonstrating your new role as a student. It may seem strange at first, but feeling strange is something that you want to generate if the placement is going to be anything more than just an extension of your working life.

We read earlier how Brenda Shapiro, a part-time student sponsored by her agency, at first resisted the role of student, but found that the idea of achieving a 'visa' for practice learning (the readiness for practice learning test) helped change her mindset. This is crucial if work-based placements are to be successful as opportunities for learning rather than a means of accrediting existing practice (▷⬚1).

Co-placements

Perhaps you are having a placement that involves more than one practice site (sometimes called 'split site'). There are many reasons why this might be the case; often it is to ensure that there is a broad enough range of opportunities for you to meet the learning requirements, if some sites are not able to meet all the occupational standards you are expected to achieve in this placement. If the placement is composed of two or more sites (as opposed to a more informal arrangement where you have a main base and take observation visits out from that principal setting), it is important that the overall placement is carefully coordinated. It works best if one site is considered to be the coordinating site, so that documentation does not fall between stools. How will you be helped to make links between the two sites, in terms of your overall learning, and who will be responsible for coordinating the arrangements for assessing your learning and practice? As long as these issues are carefully agreed, co-placements can provide an exciting opportunity for learning.

Arriving with other students

Sometimes your arrival is not as a sole visitor to the placement. There may already be social work students and ones from other professions placed there, or you may be arriving with one or more other students from the same course. This can provide a ready-made peer group which can support you during the placement. Nevertheless, there are some precautions that you should take. For example, what balance of group and individual supervision will be available (▷*Group guiding*, 112)? Will you and other students be working together on joint projects within the placement, such as co-facilitating a group for service users? If that is the case, how will individual assessments be made of the various students' contributions? The value of group placements is not in question, but the importance of making sure you are all aware of your respective responsibilities is.

Codes of practice

This chapter concerning arrival has focused on the student role, but much of the rest of the placement will focus on the *social work* role (⊠2, ⊠3). A good introduction to this can be found in the many codes of practice that have been developed for social work (⊠4). The GSCC has a code of practice for employers as well as for practitioners, and this is a useful starting point for an agency offering or considering a placement.

⊠ Click to download

⊠1 This report found very little evidence of students finding their own placements and in almost all programmes this was heavily discouraged:
  ▷ Doel, M. (2006), *Improving Practice Learning in Local Authorities 1: Developing Effective Strategies*, London: Skills for Care, 'Capturing the Learning' series www.practicelearning.org.uk

⊠2 The links between practice learning and recruitment and retention are explored in this research:
  ▷ Parker, J., Whitfield, J. and Doel, M. (2006), *Improving Practice Learning in Local Authorities 2: Workforce Planning, Recruitment and Retention*, London: Skills for Care, 'Capturing the Learning' series www.practicelearning.org.uk

⊠3 The Requirements for Social Work Training (Department of Health) in England:
  ▷ http://www.dh.gov.uk/en/Publicationsandstatistics/Publications/PublicationsPolicyAndGuidance/DH_4007803

⊠4 Codes of practice for social work can be downloaded from these
sites:
▷ GSCC Code of Practice (GSCC 2002) www.gscc.org.uk/codes
▷ British Association of Social Workers (BASW) UK (1986) www.
basw.co.uk
▷ SSSC Code of Practice (SSSC 2005), Scottish Social Services Council
www.sssc.uk.com
▷ National Association of Social Workers (NASW) US (1996, revisd
2008) www.socialworkers.org/pubs/code/default.asp
▷ International Federation of Social Workers (1988) www.ifsw.org
For *Standards for social work practice with groups*:
▷ www.aaswg.org/standards-social-work-practice-with-groups
⊠5 Teaching and learning activities, including an example of an
orientation exercise:
▷ www.shu.ac.uk/research/hsc/mswp.html

📚 Books, articles, research reports

📖1 ▷ Williams, S. and Rutter, L. (2007), *Enabling and Assessing Work-
Based Learning for Social Work: Supporting the Development of
Professional Practice*, Birmingham: Learn to Care Publication 10.
Learn to Care. www.learntocare.org.uk.
📖2 Good preparation to help you understand social work:
▷ Shardlow, S.M. and Nelson, P. (eds) (2007), *Introducing Social
Work*, Lyme Regis: Russell House Publishing.
▷ Thompson, N. (2000), *Understanding Social Work: Preparing for
Practice*, Basingstoke: Macmillan.
📖3 There is much positive practice in social work, but frequently it goes
unsung. This book tells the stories of various service users all of
whom have experienced social work positively. The authors tease out
the main learning to be derived from these stories:
▷ Doel, M. and Best, L. (2008), *Experiencing Social Work: Learning
from Service Users*, London: Sage.

CHAPTER THREE

KIT

When you set out on a journey it is always important to have the right kit with you. You need to think about the kinds of equipment and materials that will suit the journey and that will help you to get the best from it. You need to know how to use this kit, too. If you are to transform yourself from tourist to temporary resident you will need an open mind to new experiences. Supervisors also need the right kit to help them guide and test the student along the placement journey. This chapter explores the different kinds of kit available, how you can make best use of it and develop your own.

Links

Background information about your *Fellow travellers* ▷09–11.
More explanation of terms in *Language* ▷226–8.
The following topics have strong links with the themes in this chapter:
Student boundaries ▷46; *You need three legs for a stool* ▷132; *Writing up* ▷141.
Examples of placement documents are indicated by ▷**w**, and can be downloaded at: www.placementguide/routledge.

Preliminaries

'Kit' brings to mind physical stuff – reading, handbooks, computer access and the like – yet the most important bit of kit is your *mental kit*, the attitude you have and the mindset you bring to this placement journey. More than any other single factor, your mindset will determine the success of your placement; and success is not just about pass or fail but about how enjoyable it is and how much it really stretches you as a person and as a professional. So, when discussing kit with your supervisor, make sure you have the opportunity to talk about what brings you to the placement – why you want to be a social worker, for example – and what your hopes, fears and expectations are for this placement in particular.

Styles
Qualities
Rehearsal
Simulation
Reported
Observed
Live teaching
Live practice
Reflection
Networking

✦ *Chart 3.1: Putting your kit together*

Journey styles

Your approach to the placement – the *mental kit* discussed in the preliminaries – is akin to the way you might approach other aspects of living. For example, setting off on a fairly long car journey, think about which of these journey styles you favour, if any:

➢ Go with the flow, just take the routes along the way depending on what the roads are looking like, stopping off for lunch when you come across somewhere that looks OK.

➢ Get out the guides, do the research on the best route and a recommended gastro pub for lunch, and download lots of information about your final destination.

➢ Let others do the planning or leave it to the *satnav* – as long as you get there as quickly, cheaply and smoothly as possible, because the journey is something you put up with to get to the destination. Hope somebody remembers to make a packed lunch.

➢ Make sure you've got plenty to entertain you during the journey and suggest a few diversions to see some interesting sights along the way.

> ➢ Think back over similar journeys and make sure you avoid what you didn't like before and repeat some of the things you did.

TRAVELLING IN STYLE

My supervisor used 'journey styles' as an activity in our first session, so we could discuss options and see how similar and different our styles might be. At first I couldn't see the connection with my placement, but it began to click as we discussed it. I like to have things well planned, perhaps that's a consequence of being a wheelchair user, though that means I have to be very adaptable, too. It was interesting because I'd assumed we'd have to be much the same in our styles for the placement to work well, but some aspects were quite different and those are the parts I've actually enjoyed the most. I've tried to work out why and I think it's because we discussed it early on, so we often referred back to the journey styles idea and this helped me make sense of the varying *pace* of the placement and to take some risks, experiment a bit – that otherwise I would just not have felt the confidence to do.

Shama Bindana, student

Are there any other factors that would be important to you? How might your journey style differ depending on the purpose of the journey or the kind of transport you were using? Would you sometimes prefer one style and at other times another, and what might make you favour one over the others?

It is not difficult to see how these preferences would suggest radically different types of journey, even when there is a common, agreed destination. If we see the placement as a journey to achieving learning objectives, there is much to discuss about the *ways* in which the journey will be undertaken. Indeed, this is likely to play a large part in arriving safely and successfully; being aware of your preferences is an important first step.

Learning styles have been codified into a self-administered questionnaire, with four types – activist (do), reflector (review), theorist (plan and conclude) and pragmatist (respond and react) (⊠1). These are helpful as long as they are not objectified, as in 'I'm a reflector; what are you?' Indeed, one of the purposes of the placement is to stretch any habitual learning and teaching styles, not to harden and confirm them. Identifying your *learning profile* is the first step to extending it, which means considering how you might learn to use *other* styles more skilfully. Moreover, styles are not neutral; some will be more effective for a particular purpose, others more useful in other circumstances. This is true of teaching styles, too. There are good arguments to suggest that students with, say, a strong activist profile would benefit most from a placement where they learn how to strengthen other styles, not one which merely solidifies their existing approach.

STEP TO ONE SIDE

When I completed the Learning Styles questionnaire (⊠1) it wasn't a surprise to see how activist my style was, but I was shocked at how tiny my theorist and reflector style scores were. My supervisor said that as well as playing to my strengths, she wanted to help me develop these other styles, so I was better kitted out when I left the placement than when I started. I was scared of theory, but she helped me to understand more about *theorising* by using an exercise called *Unicorns* (▷89). It helped me to stop and think about what I was doing before I did it. We called this *taking a step to the left* of myself and she taught me how to visualise myself doing that. Then, she said I was to make 15 minutes for myself at the end of each placement day to think over what had happened and what my feelings were about what I'd done and learned. She said I should reflect first, then write it down as a Placement Diary (▷**W**). I visualised this as *stepping to the right* of myself. At first it all felt very strange, but I stuck at it and when I came to do the Learning Styles at the end of the placement, I was amazed that my profile had changed. It's improved my practice and my learning no end and I can see something for it.

Mary O'Connor, student

Personal qualities of students

The *mental kit* that you bring with you to the placement is bound up with your personal qualities. If you can cultivate the following four personal qualities in particular, they will stand you in good stead for the placement.

➢ **Curiosity** – 'It's great having Shama on placement because she's really interested in people and how they tick; she sees her learning as an exciting challenge, like a big jigsaw she's trying to piece together. It's been a bonus for me because looking at the work of our project through new eyes has made *me* curious again!'

John Patterson, service user supervisor.

➢ **Enthusiasm** – 'I have to say that I wasn't at all certain about this placement – it wasn't what I was looking for. But I've always been an enthusiast so I was determined to look for opportunities to stretch me, and I found them. My supervisor has told me quite a few times how much she's admired my enthusiasm – she knew this wasn't my choice of placement – and that's made me feel good about myself, too.'

Mary O'Connor, student.

➢ **Openness** – 'We've had some difficult times on the placement, but one thing that I can say held it together has been Tara's openness. She always listened to my feedback, even when it had to be very critical. I don't think we could have got through the placement without her openness – it meant I could be honest, too.'

Dave Murray, supervisor.

➢ **Take risks** – 'Nat's not afraid of tripping over, if you know what I mean. He'll try new things and take the risks that are necessary if you're going to grow. To be honest, it encouraged me, too – I was really nervous about the live teaching sessions, but seeing Nat take risks, I thought, well, I should be able to take risks, too.'

Cheryl Stone, supervisor.

A study found that humour is increasingly accepted as a strategy for coping with stress, but can humour be taught? (⏾1) What other personal qualities do you think are important to make a placement successful and which qualities do you feel you bring with you?

Rehearsal and simulation

Much of the value of a placement comes from the opportunity for live practice; in other words, to learn about practice through direct contact with people. However, like much performance, the result is improved through practice, meaning rehearsal. Evidence suggests that we need to repeat new skills many times before we become proficient at them, whether as musicians or artists, computer analysts or scientists; it is the opportunity to rehearse and repeat that leads to expertise.

Although the unique opportunity of the placement is live practice, it is rehearsal that can make the best of this opportunity. There are many ways in which this can be achieved. A discussion to prepare for contact with service users is a kind of rehearsal and this might transform into a role play in which the anticipated contact is played out beforehand.

Simulations attempt to recreate an aspect of practice, often to isolate it and thereby to focus on it. For example, a car simulator can help a learner driver's steering skills by taking care of the gears, acceleration and brakes so that the learner can concentrate on one activity at a time. Social work encounters are not so mechanical, but specific exercises and activities can focus the student's attention on one aspect at a time. Sometimes this is best done by using *parallel processes*, which help the student to step into a world which is not social work but which has parallels with social work processes. This can free both student and supervisor from *single-track thinking* – when habit closes off new ideas or solutions. Metaphor can be a creative way of bringing yourself to the situation from a very different perspective; for example, this whole guide is based on the metaphor of the placement as a journey.

✤ What if?s

What if?s are exercises that present alternative or hypothetical situations. They can help students to imagine themselves into situations that they are likely to encounter, or indeed ones that are relatively unusual yet important for them to rehearse. *What if?s* can help to isolate a particular factor, such as gender, so that the student is more aware of how it is influencing their practice: 'Ok, how might you have acted differently if she had been a man?' The *alternative doors* used in this guide are an example of *What if?s* to indicate choice and the consequences of different courses of action (▷*Being there* 67 for an example). *Student boundaries* (▷46) is an example of an entire activity made up of *What If?s* to help consider the student role in the placement (⊡2).

✤ The virtual placement

Computer-generated simulations offer whole new worlds for those who want to enter them. They make much use of the human capacity for imagination and adventure and the desire to explore worlds that can exist only in cyberspace. The learning to be gained from them can be enormous, with a strong washback to the physical world. The *Virtual Placement* (⊡3, ▷**W**) creates a virtual world in a woodland setting in which the traveller visits seven different trees (such as the *The Tree of Making Decisions*), each one posing questions, dilemmas and interactive learning. Other lives can be created in virtual worlds such as *Second Life* (⊡3), in which 'residents' can interact with each other through avatars. The potential for virtual social work in these worlds is waiting to be fully developed.

Rehearsal and simulation enable the student to go at their own pace and to repeat experiences until they feel confident with them. Of course, simulations do not substitute for direct practice but they can help students prepare for direct contact and make better sense of it.

Reported practice

Reported practice is the most common method of finding out about your practice. The requirements for *Direct observation* (▷63) ensure that these take place, but in most placements supervisors invariably rely most heavily on your own reports of your practice. Reported practice enables you to process your experience in advance of the reporting, sometimes in the form of a *process record*, in which you write not just about what happened but how you felt about what happened. It is also relatively time-saving for the supervisor, who does not have to be in the same room with you and the service users but can find out about your practice at a mutually convenient time.

RIGHT-HAND COLUMN

When students are reporting their practice in a supervision session, I think it really helps them – and it helps me – if they have processed it to a certain extent. Sometimes we do that in the session itself, but I like students to get used to doing some prep. One activity I use asks them to write down the dialogue as they can best remember it from one of the more challenging experiences they've had during the week – the sooner after the event they can do this the better. They write this down the left-hand side of the page; then on the corresponding right-hand side, in a different-coloured pen, they note what they were feeling at the time ($\triangleright\mathbf{W}$).

I tell them that this is often referred to as their 'internal monologue' and the reason why it is important to be aware of it is because it affects what they actually say and do (this is some of the learning that comes out of the exercise) and it makes for better practice if they are aware of it. This is particularly illuminating for me with students that I am supervising off-site and who I often don't get the chance to see so much in direct practice.

Dave Murray, supervisor

There are a number of shortcomings with reported practice which we explore below.

Memory

 The report relies on your memory of what happened. Even a few hours after an event your memory starts to close off certain aspects of what happened and the retelling, perhaps several days later, will suffer from the lapse of time. Any other related events between the practice and the reporting of it are also likely to alter your perception of it.

Selection

 Inevitably, your memory is selective. The amount of sensory data is such that you *have* to be selective in order to make sense of it. This means that you focus on some things and exclude others. In reported practice, your supervisor is receiving a filtered version of events and has to delve in order to try to return to events that may not have been remembered or have been selected out.

Self-awareness

 Reported practice relies on good observation skills and a high level of self-awareness; these may be the very characteristics that you are learning to acquire. People are notoriously unobservant (⌂4) and it is not realistic to expect that your account to your supervisor will be entirely neutral.

Snapshot

Practice experiences that are reported after the event are more like a series of photographic snapshots than a moving film. Although these can evoke a story, they tend to be sketchy and episodic and leave the listener to fill in the details and make the connections between the various episodes.

Reported practice relies on considerable trust that, even if you are aware of all that is happening in your practice, you feel confident enough to share difficulties, anxieties – and indeed positives – with your supervisor. No matter how honest you wish to be, reported practice is mediated by what you feel is appropriate to share. Exercises like *Right-hand column* (▷61) can help to expose these feelings, but direct observation and live teaching are important to provide a more rounded picture, as we will now explore.

Direct observation

There is a requirement for direct observation of the student, ranging from a minimum of three occasions in England and Scotland to six in Wales. Direct observation helps to counter the limitations mentioned earlier in connection with reported practice. First, it does not rely solely on one person's memory. Second, though the observer will also be selective, there is every chance that the observer's selectiveness will differ from the student's in some respects so that, together, there is a fuller picture. The observer, as an experienced practitioner, will be more aware of what to look for in the practice situation and less emotionally and personally involved, and so can observe the situation from a relatively detached perspective ($\triangleright$**W**).

Direct observation should not take place without agreeing ground rules:

➢ Who will decide which observations will be made and when?
➢ How will the service users' meaningful consent to the direct observation be ensured?
➢ How will the supervisor be introduced and the purpose of the observation explained to the service users?
➢ Under what circumstances might the supervisor intervene in the observation (for example, if you are providing inaccurate information to the service user)?
➢ How will the findings from the observation be recorded, discussed and assessed?

Consider an example of how Dave Murray uses observations for learning, practice development and assessment ($\triangleright$*You need three legs for a stool*, 132).

Schedule a supervision session as soon as possible after the direct observation. Your memories will be fresh and any difficulties can be talked over immediately so that they do feel that they are hanging over you like a cloud.

Live teaching

Direct observation has much to offer, but if it is just a question of the observer 'parachuting in' to watch the student's practice this can feel intrusive or disruptive. It is also a wasted opportunity because direct observation can be transformed into a more active engagement with the student and the service users through *live teaching* (◈2). Similar methods are used in some family therapy settings (where a one-way mirror and earphones may be deployed) and we will consider a variant for student supervision shortly. First, let us explore some of the advantages of teaching the student live in the company of service users.

Modelling

 The apprenticeship model sought to reproduce the supervisor's practice in that of the supervisee and, rightly, that model fell out of fashion. However, we should not underestimate the role that the supervisor has to play as an experienced practitioner to whom students look as a model of practice. Being there in the room with the student and service users enables the supervisor to model certain aspects of practice (open questioning, for instance).

Immediate feedback

If you were learning how to knit and you dropped a stitch it would be much more helpful to have someone tell you there and then that the stitch had been dropped rather than carry on knitting, only to have to unravel it all a few days later in your 'knitting supervision session'. So, there are enormous benefits from having a direct and instant feedback loop, which is possible when the practice teacher is there in the presence of the student (▷*Feedback*, 72).

Support

Staying with the knitting analogy, it can feel more supportive to have someone able to pick up the dropped stitch and help you with it there and then. Supervisors might feel it is supportive to help students unravel it later, but in fact this could be experienced as rather demoralising. There is support in being able to build on the student's good practice, too. Indeed, when the student's practice is very good, live teaching can become *co-working*, whilst being open about power differentials, of course

Assessment

Live teaching helps the supervisor to evaluate the strengths and weaknesses of the student's practice. It is likely to be a more accurate assessment than reported practice; if you were to assess a pianist's skills on the basis of their description of the way they gave a performance that you had not heard, you would think this a strange way to come to a judgement. Live teaching can provide rich material for the student's portfolio and for the supervisor's assessment report

Quality

Live teaching helps assure the quality of the service that people are receiving from students. In direct observation, what do you do when you have concerns about the direction the student is taking? Live teaching gives permission to intervene in various ways that can provide not just immediate learning for the student but also protection for the service users. It can also be the backdrop for a more meaningful contribution by service users to an evaluation of the student's work.

Aid to indirect teaching

The experiences that are gathered through live teaching provide lots of additional material for subsequent indirect teaching in the supervision session. You can point the student in the direction of particular exercises and articles to prepare for the session, in the light of what happened in the live teaching session; you can prepare *what if?* scenarios and rehearsals to use in supervision (▷60). You can feel confidence that all of these will be relevant because of your direct experience of the practice to which they will refer.

Credentials

Students need to have confidence that their supervisors are skilled practitioners. Watching you in action, via some of the interventions in live teaching, can develop the student's respect for your practice. The practice need only be skilled, not superlative, since the latter

could feel too distant from the student's range – like watching a highly skilled knitter produce a complex, ribbed cardigan in a matter of minutes!

Model to introduce direct observation and live teaching

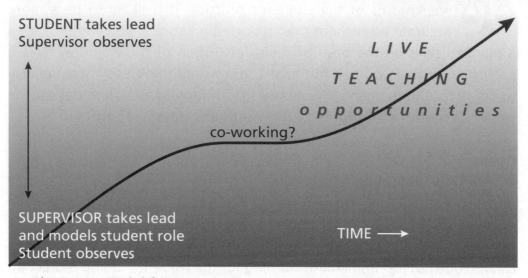

STUDENT takes lead
Supervisor observes

LIVE

TEACHING

opportunities

co-working?

SUPERVISOR takes lead
and models student role
Student observes

TIME ⟶

✦ *Chart 3.2: Model for introducing direct observation and live teaching*

Live teaching is more likely to be successful if it is introduced in a systematic way as part of a carefully constructed model. Chart 3.2 shows the placement running over time from left to right; early on, the student observes the supervisor's practice on a regular basis. This is the opportunity for the supervisor to model the student role, the kind of behaviour that will be expected of the student, with the supervisor introducing the student to a fair and systematic model of *Feedback* (▷72) and demonstrating the openness and reflection that will be expected of the student.

DOOR 1   BEING THERE   DOOR 2

DOOR 1

As a part-time student on a distance-learning programme, with placements in my own agency, I had insisted that I have an external supervisor, Dave Murray. At first I found Dave a bit intimidating. He was quite intense with high standards of practice – would I ever be able to match them? But he reassured me that he respected the fact that I was an experienced worker, but that I was also a student (it took me a while to see this as a positive label). The turning point for me was when he put himself in the position of the student – I observed him and gave *him* feedback. He taught me a system for live teaching which made me less nervous than I thought I would be when it came to my turn to be observed by him, because I knew the rules and that he was there to support me. I'm not saying it didn't feel strange – it felt really different to what I normally do – but I was surprised that this felt like a good thing. I felt the adrenalin afterwards!

Brenda Shapiro, student

DOOR 2

There'd been a suggestion of some outside supervisor watching me, but fortunately it didn't happen. I was very relieved – it's such an artificial situation. I don't know how they could have expected to get the 'real me'. I think my agency was pleased, too – more expense and complicated. So my line manager did the observations. We get on fine, but I was more nervous than I thought I would be, because he doesn't generally see me actually with service users. And we had to cancel one session because there was an emergency he had to deal with. He gave me general feedback afterwards that was fine and pretty much what I'd expected. It felt a bit of an anticlimax, but I'm a well-established member of the team so there's nothing new to add, is there? I couldn't really see the point in putting us all through this time-consuming activity. I guess it's to check that I'm doing what I say I'm doing, going through the hoops.

Brenda Shapiro, student

Gradually, the student takes increasing responsibility until they are providing the lead. The timescale (i.e. the period of time that is covered in Chart 3.2) will vary from student to student and this will be a good indication of the student's progress. In many cases, but not all, there can be a period during which there is a balance between the student taking the lead and the supervisor taking the lead, akin to co-working. The possibility of co-working, with student and supervisor sharing the lead in direct work with service users, is a good indicator of satisfactory progress by the student (▷*Chart 7.2*, 150).

Live teaching is introduced in the period when the student is taking the greater responsibility for leading. As part of this kind of systematic model, live teaching is not seen as a special event, but as part of a pattern of working together in which supervisors have already shown themselves open about their own practice and have modelled methods of feedback that are fair and honest.

This model needs adaptation for *off-site* supervision, where the supervisor does not have regular contact with the student. Direct observation and live teaching are likely to be experienced as special events when there has not been the opportunity for the student to observe the off-site supervisor's practice on a regular basis. In these circumstances, it is worth considering how the on-site supervisor can be trained to perform live teaching.

Rules for live teaching

Live teaching should be conducted carefully and within agreed rules. Once the general model to introduce direct observation and live teaching is understood, the options that are available during the live teaching experience need to be discussed with all involved – including, of course, the service users. Before any live teaching can take place, service users must give informed consent based on their understanding of clear and open explanations of the purpose of the live teaching, and with the knowledge that they can withdraw consent at any time. Anecdotal evidence suggests that service users benefit from the experience of live teaching, though the formal evidence base needs to be developed.

There are four possible actions during the live teaching, any one of which might be used any number of times during the session.

1   **The supervisor can address the student directly** – e.g. a suggestion that the student pursue a certain line or a question that helps illuminate what is happening for the student.

2   **The supervisor can address the service users directly** – e.g. a specific question directed to the service users, or perhaps a reflection that is intended to help them to see the situation differently.

3   **The supervisor can address the process** – a statement or comment is made about what is happening but this comment is not directed at any one particular person.

4   **Time out** is called to give the opportunity for the supervisor and student to talk somewhere away from the service users, and indeed for the service users to talk away from the professionals. In theory, anyone can call for time out, though it is most likely to be the supervisor.

Of course, there is also a fifth course of action:

5   **Do nothing** – this should be a positive choice not simply a default setting.

GOING LIVE

I was resistant to this live teaching when my supervisor first talked about it early in the placement. But, by the time we came to do it, I'd seen her quite a few times in direct practice and I felt more confident. It was still very strange, but then I figured that if I'm truly going to be stretched in my learning it *should* feel strange. It didn't feel unsupportive, in fact I think it was very supportive, just a bit self-conscious.

It was important to debrief soon after the session, not just about its content and learning I got from the live teaching, but also the process. This meant that I felt more in control of what would happen next time and I could tell the supervisor which of her interventions worked best and which not so well. I've found that it's also important that the service users have an opportunity right at the end of the session to say how they found it and to ask them whether and how they feel it made a difference to their experience. They tend to say a bit the same as me – it was a bit strange but they enjoyed it and they got a lot from it.

Nat Davies, student

The live teaching session is rather like *Sliding Doors*, the film in which the difference between catching a train and not catching a train has a huge impact on the course of a person's life (⊠5). In common with the 'doors' blogs in this guide (*Being there* is an example, ▷67), live teaching rests on the premise that there are significant choices, in this case throughout each session with service users, about what to ask, when and how. Proceduralised practice, encouraged by formalised assessment schedules, limits these kinds of choice by imposing a template on the intervention. Professional practice seeks to expand these choices. Live teaching is an opportunity for the supervisor to model 'sliding doors' with decisions to make about when and whether to intervene, and how; it is also an opportunity to develop professional, rather than routinised, practices.

Live practice

There are some placements, notably with community organisations and in daycare and residential settings, where much of what you do is observed, formally or informally, because of the nature of the setting. However, for many students, the journey through *Socialworkland* is likely to be solo, with trips out with the supervisor only for special occasions, such as a direct observation. Of course, there are other people where you are placed who might also be able to show you *Socialworkland*, and they will each give you a different perspective on what you see.

Learning from live practice is an intriguing mix of careful planning, so you know what you are looking for, and serendipitous happenings along the way. Discuss how you can achieve the best mix with your supervisor and aim to see how they achieve this balance in their own work, no matter how experienced a traveller, there are always new developments and circumstances, so check out what 'the locals' do.

Live practice is more than the experience itself; it is what you have learned from this experience. How are you going to capture and process this learning? Again, it is important to learn ways in which you can bring back the knowledge, experience and learning that arises from your live practice. You need kit not just to get around, but to keep a hold of what you find – in particular, you will need to be able to retrieve these findings in order to demonstrate your growing abilities ($\triangleright$*Testing competence*, 129). Out and about in *Socialworkland*, the challenge is not in the finding, but in the sampling: how to decide what is worth bringing back, what will count as an accurate sample of your learning and practice ($\triangleright$*What is evidence?* 125). A thorough knowledge of the National Occupational Standards is essential, along with guidance from your supervisor about how the standards relate to the kinds of activity in *this* particular practice site. The geologists' equivalent is knowing they must find particular fossil examples; first, they need to know what to look for and second, they need to know where best to look for them. Until they are experienced enough just to *know*, a guidebook would be useful, showing the difference between an ammonite and a belemnite, for example. Until you know the occupational standards backwards, make sure you have a copy of them to hand, along with the skeleton of your portfolio, so you can begin to collect experiences that illustrate learning objectives and standards.

◊ Feedback

Giving and receiving feedback is a critical part of the placement kit. Positive feedback should be given regularly to reinforce positive attitudes, skills and attributes (such as perseverance) – these should not just be taken for granted. Some feedback is aimed at helping students to improve certain aspects of their practice. In these cases, the more immediate feedback can be the better, so it should follow closely on the event. Timing is one of the most important, but overlooked, aspects of good feedback. More reflective feedback is probably better left to mature. This is most true when the feedback might be especially critical and more general or less obvious: for example, if the supervisor is uncertain about the student's attitude to some of the service users. In most circumstances the supervisor will want to check to see if there is a pattern and aim to give feedback that will help to change it.

Feedback should be two-way, so that supervisors regularly ask for feedback from students about their experience of the placement in general and the supervision in particular. Of course, there are power differentials between the student and the supervisor and these should be discussed openly. In many ways, this is good modelling for the way the student will ask for feedback from service users, where there are similar power imbalances. An early supervision session should discuss how feedback will be sought from service users in a fair and regular fashion and how it will incorporate a measure of independence (▷*Service user feedback*, 212).

Feedback is not an opportunity for a generalised moan. That is why it is really important for the ground rules for feedback to be established early on. Feedback should:

➢ focus on behaviours, attitudes and skills – not on the person
➢ be focused and specific rather than generalised

➢ be forward-looking, in terms of how things might be changed
➢ balance positive feedback around strengths and critical feedback around what needs to change
➢ not be an opportunity to ventilate strong feelings, but an invitation to dialogue
➢ give consideration to the timing of the feedback.

It is the impact of feedback that is important. Has the behaviour or attitude changed as a result of feedback and consequent discussion? For this reason, you should always review the feedback after some time to see what difference it has made to the situation.

Reflection

The importance of reflection in and on practice is well-documented (≋3): but where do you find the space for reflection and how are you going to ensure that it is a permanent feature of your map and not a temporary structure? Group activity (whether for students or supervisors) is one way to commit yourself to saving time for reflection. It should be *critical* reflection, and as such might not be compatible with some organisational cultures. The pressures of bureaucracies to enforce rule-governed behaviour is a tension that research suggests influences practitioners considerably (≋4), yet the view that reflective practice is a luxury we can't afford is not compatible with good social work practice. The placement is an excellent place to get into the habit of reflecting critically on your work and also developing strategies to keep the habit when you are a busy practitioner.

REFLECTIVE ACCOUNT

I first learned about reflective accounts on the three-day course to prepare me for work-based supervision. I told myself that I couldn't expect the student to do something that I hadn't done myself (how would I *really* know what it should look like?) At first I found it very hard to find the time and I just got to putting it off. Then we started up this group for supervisors, we meet every two weeks and they said: 'Make an appointment with yourself.' So I do, write it in my diary and keep it safe. And I make sure my student does, too. The supervisors' group also gives me a purpose for my reflective account, a kind of audience that I keep in mind when I'm writing it. At first I was a bit 'I did this, then I did that' and they told me straight that they needed to know more about *me*, it wasn't meant to be a newspaper report, but something I could open myself up to, about what I was feeling about my practice (and the supervision of the student sometimes figured) and what I was learning from it and how I was doing things differently. It all helped me to help the students shape their reflective accounts, because they started off just the same, being too descriptive. They like it, that I do reflective accounts, too.

Cheryl Stone, supervisor

▷*Wisdom of the group*, 137, to consider an example of the kind of support Cheryl Stone's supervisors' group gives.

Social networking

Some courses provide interactive facilities, such as chatrooms and electronic discussion groups. You might find that your greatest support comes from other students. If you are a full-time student your opportunities for face-to-face contact are likely to be greater than, say, if you are studying part time or on a distance programme. In these circumstances the chance to keep in touch using other means can be very welcome. Social networking is one way of having contact with students who may be separated by distance. There are online services, such as Ning

(⌂6), that help you create, customise and share a social network. Topic threads can be followed, with new topics introduced as people wish. Some courses are experimenting with this kind of communication. It is important to discuss questions of confidentiality and how information on the network might be used, whoever creates the social network – the course, a supervisor, students themselves.

On-line discussion forums are hosted by 'Community Care' on a variety of topics and there is a specific forum for students. A typical posting (⌂7):

THREADS

Anyone else in placement atm? I am currently in a children's placement, a community development project. I am in the process of setting up a safe kids project with a group of children, using referrals received from the social services. Some of the background to the children was heart breaking and it makes me realise quite what professionals in children's services might come across on a daily basis. Do they become hardened to it? It was really hard reading. And I am anticipating that it will be difficult running the safe kids sessions on a neutral basis, it might be tricky knowing their history as I do. It will be valuable experience and a challenge.

⌂ Click to download

⌂1 The Honey and Mumford Learning Styles questionnaire:
      ▷ www.peterhoney.com/

⌂2 The Scottish Organisation for Practice Teaching (ScOPT) has developed a compendium of activities for supervisors and students:
      ▷ Practice Learning and Teaching: Tools for the Job, compiled by
         Penny Forshaw and Theresa Cowe www.scopt.co.uk

⌂3 The Virtual Placement ▷ www.routledge.com/textbooks/9780415499125
      Second life ▷ www.secondlife.com

⌂4 The 'opaque gorilla' from Simons and Chabris:
      ▷ viscog.beckman.uiuc.edu/flashmovie/15.php

The instructions need to be read first and followed through for this experiment in observation to work.

'Gorillas in our midst: sustained inattentional blindness for dynamic events':

▷ www.wjh.harvard.edu/~cfc/Simons1999.pdf

⌂5 Information about 'Sliding Doors' ▷ www.imdb.com/title/tt0120148/

⌂6 Ning is an example of a social networking online service:
▷ www.ning.com

⌂7 Community care discussion forums, including the students':
▷ www.communitycare.co.uk/carespace/forums/

📚 Books, articles, research reports

📚1 Moran, C.C. and Hughes, L.P. (2006), 'Coping with stress: social work students and humour', *Social Work Education*, 25:5, pp501–17.

📚2 An early text on live teaching/supervision:
▷ Evans, D. (1087), 'Live supervision in the same room: practice teaching method', *Social Work Education*, 6:3, pp13–16

📚3 The foremost text on reflective practice:
▷ Schon, D. (1983), *The Reflective Practitioner: how professionals think in action*, London: Temple Smith.

Other useful texts about reflection and reflective practice:
▷ Brookfield, S.D. (1995), *Becoming a Critically Reflective Teacher*, San Francisco: Jossey Bass.
▷ Gould, N. and Taylor, I. (eds) (1996), *Reflective Learning for Social Work*, Aldershot: Ashgate.
▷ Moon, J. A. (2004), *A Handbook of Reflective and Experiential Learning*, Oxford: Routledge.
▷ Thompson, S. and Thompson, N. (2008), *The Critically Reflective Practitioner*, Basingstoke: PalgraveMacmillan.
▷ Yelloly, M., and Henkle, M. (eds) (1995), *Learning and Teaching in Social Work: Towards Reflective Practice*, London: Jessica Kingsley.

📚4 Research into student's readiness for practice revealed the strength of organisational culture on new workers:
▷ Marsh, P. and Triseliotis, J. (1996), *Ready to Practice? Social Workers and Probation Officers: Their Training and First Year in Work*, Aldershot: Avebury.

5 A key text for skill development:

▷ Trevithick P. (2006), *Social Work Skills. A Practice Handbook* (2nd edition), Maidenhead: Open University Press.

Some other texts that focus on skill development, adult learning and professional development:

▷ Brown R. and Rutter L. (2006), *Critical Thinking for Social Work*, Maidstone: Learning Matters.

▷ Doel M. and Shardlow S. (2005), *Modern Social Work Practice: Teaching and Learning in Practice Settings*, Aldershot: Ashgate

▷ Hillier, Y. (2002), *Reflective Teaching in Further and Adult Education*, London: Continuum.

▷ Honey, P. (1988), *Face to Face: A Practical Guide to Interactive Skills* (2nd edition), Aldershot: Gower.

▷ Honey, P. and Mumford, A. (1995), *Using Your Learning Styles* (3rd edition), Berkshire: Peter Honey.

CHAPTER FOUR

MAPPING

Orientation is an activity that starts to make sense of a new experience (▷48). It is the first step in a wider process of mapping which helps to identify the central features, to locate them in relation to one another, and even to create your own maps – mental maps that can change the way you look at the world. Maps can give you theoretical knowledge of places that you have not actually visited, which means that you can prepare yourself to get the best out of the placement experience. The placement is often described as an opportunity for students to integrate theory and practice, yet this is frequently presented as highly problematic, an artificial activity in which, as the student, you have the laborious task of translating the 'theory language' learned in college into the 'practice language' spoken on placement, as if you need a kind of dictionary. If you are taught two separate languages, of course you will spend time struggling to translate between the two. The notion of mapping will help you chart a course so as to get to grips, both with the curriculum for the placement and with the relationship between theory and practice. The guide aims to make it less mystifying by considering concrete examples of how you theorise about practical, about practice wisdom, hypothesis-making and judgement in social work.

Links

Background information about your *Fellow travellers* ▷09–11.
More explanation of terms in *Language* ▷226–8.
The following topics have strong links with the themes in this chapter:
▷*National Occupational Standards* 19; ▷*Orientation* 48; ▷*Reflection* 73;
▷*Professional conduct* 134; ▷*Testing values* 136.
This chapter makes reference to the map of *Socialworkland* ▷xviii–xix.
Examples of placement documents are indicated by ▷**w**, and can be downloaded at: www.routledge.com/textbooks/9780415499125

Preliminaries

It will be helpful for you to map your placement against the specific learning objectives that have been identified in your Learning Agreement (▷24). If we can continue with our travel metaphor, you are more than a visitor to *Socialworkland* – you must discover how the various features of the placement landscape relate to the requirements for your learning. So, no matter how pleasant it might be to stick around in one part, you will need to be adventurous in order to cover the ground. This will mean being open to experiences that are not always within your comfort zone and that is why 'mapping' is important, so that you can prepare yourself and help your supervisor to prepare you. It will also help you to gauge just how much territory there is to survey so you do not find yourself running out of time on placement. You will also need to relate *Socialworkland* to your existing experiences, perhaps to a previous placement (▷*From placement to placement*, 193).

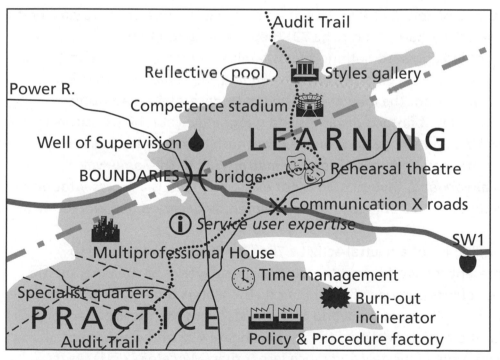

✦ *Chart 4.1: Practice-learning twin cities*

Practice curriculum

The map of *Socialworkland* (▷xviii–xix) in the introduction to the guide beckons us to a landscape in which various features are identified. We are invited to see social work as something that can be mapped, even associated with physical features such as lakes and mountains, cities and townships. This identification of features is pretty much what a *curriculum* does: it outlines the content for learning, and groups this content into units and modules of associated topics. The practice of developing a curriculum is commonplace in educational settings such as the universities and colleges that offer social work education, but it is not how practitioners see their practice. This is one of the differences that practitioners experience as they become teachers of practice – they have to find ways of describing the landscape that they have taken for granted so they can help others to learn about it (☙1).

The map of *Socialworkland* is not 'real', nor is the one of the 'twin cities' depicted in Chart 4.1 on page 79. They are designed to provoke a new way of looking at something that is familiar, a kind of *simulation* (▷59). They are perhaps best described as *simulacrum*, something that is a representation. The map of the London Underground is an iconic simulacrum: it distorts distances and geography, yet it helps visitors to move around a huge and complex city much more readily than an accurate map (▷*Practice-Learning metro*, 172). In the same way, *Socialworkland*, though it does not exist as a place, is a representation of the features that will need to be explored, understood and worked with.

Mapping is not a neutral activity. The way in which we choose to represent the world (be it the outer physical world, or the inner mental one) reflects our way of looking at it. The 'Peters projection' gives a very different picture of the world than the standard Mercator projection, with the former depicting the proportionate size of the continent of Africa more accurately and much larger than Mercator's (⬚1). As it stands, the map of *Socialworkland* in the guide's introduction is relatively euro-centric in its representation; an afro-centric map of social work could look quite different, both in the physical features it uses as representations and also the aspects of social work that are identified. The representation of social work could also take place at different levels, as we will discuss in the following section.

Specialist practice

There is a tension in social work education that plays itself out in the relationship between placements and class-based teaching. This revolves around the fact that the award for which you are studying provides a general social work qualification, yet the placements that you experience will be in specialist settings. This is not a fatal tension, but it is one that should be openly acknowledged. In this way, as a supervisor, you can better understand the difference between what you do as a practitioner (a mental health social worker, for example) and what you do as a practice teacher (an educator guiding the student's learning about social work – not training them to become a mental health practitioner).

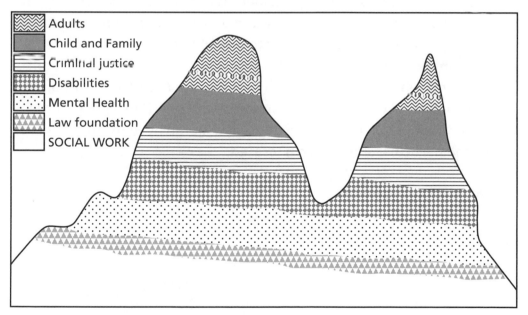

+ Chart 4.2: Sectional map of Socialworkland

Socialworkland is a general map of features common to all social work, so where does specialist practice fit in this map? In Chart 4.1 it is portrayed as occupying separate quarters in Practice City. Depending on your view of specialist practice vis-à-vis generalist practice, you might refer to these quarters more as ghettoes, because of the dangers that different branches of social work will build walls between themselves which become so high that they induce separate development. It is paradoxical that at a time of much rhetoric about dismantling barriers *between* professions, social work risks disaggregation into specialist enclaves. The separate development of social work and probation work, for example, was a direct result of the separation of the education of these two professional groups. Any move to separate the education of the different social work specialisms would almost certainly see the end of social work as we know it.

Another kind of mapping is geological. Instead of focusing on the surface features, we take a section through the rock on which these features sit. This encourages us to conceptualise social work practice as an entity (the foundation rock) with different strata visible on various parts of its surface. In other words, if your placement is in a disabilities team, you are part of the general social work landscape but the section which is exposed to you in this case is specific to disabilities. So, the geological simulacrum for *Socialworkland* might look something like Chart 4.2 on page 81. This representation also includes the *law foundation* strata, to suggest that social work practice is based on a sound knowledge of the legal foundations. There is no intention of a hierarchy in terms of where any of the particular specialisms is located.

GENERALIST AND GENERIC

In the module Preparation for Placement, we aim to help the students get a clear understanding of the differences between specialist, generalist and generic practice. 'Specialist' they have no problem with – pretty much every setting they are going to is now specialist (child and families, adults, mental health, criminal justice and the like). 'Generic' we say is what all these specialist practices have in common that makes them 'social work' – core values, skills and knowledge. 'Generalist' practice is hard to find these days, but patchwork and community social work were good examples of these, where social workers worked with a wide range of people in the community, rather like a general practitioner, a kind of social practitioner! These are more than just words, they are important concepts that help students understand what social work is – and can be.

Sandra Townsend, director of practice studies

Personalising your map

Whether it is represented as a map or listed as a set of bullet points, the practice curriculum is expressed at a general level. As soon as you arrive at the actual placement you will need to relate these general features to the particular topography of the practice site. The practice curriculum is something abstract, but now you are faced with the practical reality of how to engage with these features – the values, the cultural competence, the practice methods, the decision-making and so on. Moreover, this landscape is *peopled* by colleagues, other professionals and those who use the services, all of whom have an impact on how you experience it.

PRIME LOCATION

When my community group started to offer placements with me as a work-based supervisor I didn't know how we'd do it really, me not being a social worker. Then, when I saw *Socialworkland* I could see how what we did at our project could match what students needed to learn about, even though we never called it 'social work' as such. We started at the Pond of Doubt – a strange place to start, maybe! But it came out of both of us feeling how we'd always seen doubt as something to conquer (we both had our own demons) but how, actually, it was a positive thing, too. On the map, it's near to the swamps of risk-taking and the bridge of decision-making, and townships like Empowerment and Judgement – we could match it all to Tara's competences and the units. And it was good fun, too.

John Patterson, service user provider

I couldn't see what the map thing could mean for my placement but I was lucky that my work-based supervisor had a good imagination and he used it to show how I could achieve my key roles, like Unit 12 which is 'Assess and manage risks'. We looked at how your doubts 'that drain down into the swamp' are actually OK because they force you to look for stepping stones through the swamp – you test yourself and think carefully. I got a sort of videoclip in my mind, like I'd taken it on my mobile, each time I needed to make a decision, of what my doubts were, what the stepping stones were, at what point I'd be ready to cross the bridge to make a decision and how to make sure that the service user and me were always together, me listening to them and them to me so we crossed the swamp safely!

Tara Watson, student

From the beginning of the placement you and your supervisor are relating your personal learning objectives, spelled out in the *Learning agreement* (▷24), to the key roles as set out in the *National occupational standards* (▷19). The *Socialworkland* map can help to provide the bigger picture, but the supervisor helps the student to recognise and use the specific opportunities that this particular placement provides. In effect, you are learning how to do your own mapping, but this time the map is of your own personal journey into the landscape – what and how you learned and how you gathered evidence of this along the way, a kind of video diary. More of this in *Guiding* (▷100–118) and *Testing* (▷119–146).

Two vocabularies?

Let us remind ourselves that placements occupy half of the course and class-based studies comprise the other half. Both halves work best when they are properly connected; it is one course, not two. Despite this, there is often a temptation to see the placement as the real work and the time spent in class as academic in the pejorative sense of that word: that is, not especially relevant. This is a mistake. Social work is a wonderful mix of practical skills, value judgements and well-developed powers of thought used to arrive at fine-tuned judgements. A responsible practitioner is one who is concerned to develop their practical, ethical and intellectual skills and to find ways of adding to the profession's knowledge.

The reality is that not every workplace is so open to intellectual ideas. You will meet some practitioners with polarised beliefs – that you are either good at practice or at the theory, but not the two. In fact, the two are interdependent and it is difficult to think of practice being 'good' if it is separated from rigorous thinking and theorising, just as a good social work theory must surely be capable of finding expression in practice, as a practical theory.

It is reasonable to suppose that supervisors are less likely to be anti-intellectual since the motivation to supervise often embraces a critical interest in practice and genuine enquiry into what makes it 'tick', and therefore an openness to the importance of thinking as well as doing. The mapping activities which we have been discussing in this chapter illustrate the attempt to encourage conceptualisation and to hitch this to practical realities.

TOUR: DICTIONARY

A common course divided by two languages?

ACADEMISH	AGENCISH
as·sess·ment *n.*	**as·sess·ment** *n.*
A method of evaluating student performance and attainment.	A judgment about something based on an understanding of the situation.
prac·tise *vti.*	**prac·tice** *n.*
To do something repeatedly in order to improve performance.	A habit, custom, or usual way of doing something.
the·o·ry *n.*	**re·al·i·ty** *n.*

ACADEMISH — **the·o·ry** *n.*

1. The body of rules, ideas, principles, and techniques that applies to a particular subject, especially when seen as distinct from actual practice.
2. Abstract thought or contemplation.
3. An idea of or belief about something arrived at through speculation or conjecture.
4. A set of circumstances or principles that is hypothetical.
5. A set of facts, propositions, or principles analysed in their relation to one another and used to explain phenomena.

AGENCISH — **re·al·i·ty** *n.*

1. Actual being or existence, as opposed to an imaginary, idealized, or false nature.
2. Everything that actually does or could exist or happen in real life.
3. Something that has real existence and must be dealt with in real life.
4. A kind of existence or universe, either connected with or independent from other kinds.
5. The totality of real things in the world, independent of people's knowledge or perception of them.

One of the main challenges for supervisors is to speak both languages, helping the student to translate and integrate the vocabularies of academy and agency, and ensuring that the agency understands the different position that the student occupies in relation to employees. This is especially important for those students who are *also* employees (▷199). The notion of the two vocabularies can help people to realise these differences, which is the first step to reconciling them.

Pet theories

The difficulty that is so commonly experienced in 'integrating theory and practice' is ironic given that attempts to separate theory and practice are illusory: you theorise all the time. These working hypotheses may not be consciously based on formally tested theories, but they are nonetheless examples of theorising and they are significant because they drive your actions. The placement is a somewhere to bring these *pet theories* to the surface so they can be tested rigorously; it is an opportunity to make sure that your professional activity is not based on whim or habit.

When pet theories enter broader circulation and gain greater credence within any group, such as a professional group, we often refer to them as *practice wisdom*. The wisdom that arises from the experience of practice is important and may well have stood the test of time. However, you do not have to believe that evidence only comes from the scientific rigour of a randomised controlled trial (RCT) (⊡2) to be concerned that practice wisdom should be properly scrutinised. Whatever the evidence base for the practice wisdom, it should be open and explicit so that others can judge fairly whether it has been put to the test. Everyday aphorisms (pet theories shared by a wider community or people) can be used to justify unethical positions. For example, 'spare the rod and spoil the child' was used without any substantiating evidence to justify behaviour that would now be described as physical abuse.

CHECKPOINT THEORY

I've always been comfortable with ideas and formal theory – did philosophy as an undergraduate, but I'd sort of disconnected the -*ism*s of my studies from the practical work. It wasn't that I saw them as incompatible, just somehow not related, not relevant to one another. Also, when I did get into the -*ism*s I guess I'd tend to over-intellectualise. My supervisor didn't let me get away with this! She didn't challenge me head-on, but said that she wanted me to do some direct observations of her and others in the team, and one of the things she wanted me to look out for was what she called 'informal theorising' – pet theories, if you like, examples of people's reasoning and how or whether it linked to any of the grander theories (those that started with a capital letter!) that I was familiar with. I wasn't so sure about this, but once I got going there was no stopping me – theorising was like breathing, impossible not to do. I really enjoyed linking it to the grander theories – sociological, psychological, philosophical – too. My supervisor asked me to share my observations and analyses with the team, which I was a bit nervous about, but it went well and everyone got a lot from it. I was grateful to my supervisor because I feel she was playing to my strengths. At first I reckoned I'd given rather more than I'd got, but I was wrong, because this activity – she called it *Checkpoint Theory* – forced me to make the links that I had been avoiding, or at least missing, in my own practice. I still tend to intellectualise but now I'm OK to make the links with day-to-day practice and check how this theorising drives what I do, and be critical of it.

Nat Davies, student

Travellers' stories

Pet theory, local wisdom and the like are not confined to the vocabulary of agency life. No doubt there are some interesting examples of theorising doing the rounds of your course, as students exchange views, opinions and hypotheses that have been triggered either directly from placement experience, or from other aspects of the social work programme. Sometimes these are singular events that make a good tale, but at other times they start to snowball; generalisations are made from a cluster of separate experiences that seem to justify a hypothesis which in turn can harden into course wisdom. Look out for these and make a note of them in your Placement diary (▷33). Try to track down their origins and put them through an 'evidence test' – what is the evidence that might corroborate or challenge them? Are they a variant of the urban myth – *a course myth* – or do they have a solid basis? What other purposes might these pet theories serve?

UNICORNS

Once I started to look, the air was thick with them – pet theories. My best friend, she's mad on horses, and she even gave these theories a pet name – *Unicorns*. She said you had to assume they weren't really true until you could prove it. One that was in the air was that the course was treating us younger students more strictly than the mature students and that they, the older ones, were having an easier time of it, especially those that had placements where they were working. Without this *unicorn* idea we would just've moaned about it, but we started to think about how it related to ageism, which we'd done in the social inclusion module. Most people think of old ageism, but we were relating it to youth ageism at personal, cultural and structural levels. We overheard one of the older students referring to the younger ones as 'babies'. We made it into a game, seeing if there was evidence to turn our hypothetical unicorn into an actual horse. I'm still not sure about this one, but I'm enjoying thinking about what is evidence and what can be proved. I've learned how to be sceptical and turn things over – it's helped me on placement.

Tara Watson, student

Evidence-based practice

Evidence-based practice (EBT) has become the accepted orthodoxy for professional practice. In some respects it is difficult to think what else practice could or should be based on: *whim*-based practice? However, despite its seemingly self-evident nature, it does raise many questions and it is contentious. The first question is *whose* evidence? How do the experiences of people who use social work become part of the evidence base? Other related questions are *what* counts as evidence and *how* is the evidence to be gathered? The randomised controlled trial (RCT) (⌂2) is the gold standard used by the physical sciences and medicine. However, there have been few RCTs in social work in the UK, so that would rather limit the evidence available to us, even if there was agreement that knowledge derived from RCTs deserved a privileged position in social work.

As well as fears that EBT can exclude important areas of knowledge and experience from the *evidence camp*, there are concerns that it crowds out diversity in practice. For example, there is a growing use of groupwork-by-manual, which requires groupworkers to follow a highly prescribed programme that has been sanctioned as evidence based through earlier trials. Undoubtedly, these programmes are generally a good basis from which to start; however, the evidence that is missing (because it is not being gathered) is knowledge about how far it is the practitioner's skill *as a groupworker* that counts, or whether anybody can take the manual off the shelf and facilitate a successful group. Groupworkers who used to create their own programmes are now increasingly finding that this is no longer an option and that they must follow tightly controlled programmes, these days usually based on cognitive behavioural treatments, written by others. So, instead of encouraging an environment in which agencies and practitioners are genuinely curious to experiment to find out what works (which is surely the philosophy of evidence-based practice), EBT is seen by some as sanctioning an orthodoxy that stunts experiment and, ironically, delivers a less professionalised service.

Lastly, cynicism about evidence-based practice is fed by the knowledge that there is plenty of evidence that is entirely overlooked because it is inconvenient, either because it is expensive, would be unpopular with the public, or runs counter to the government's current obsession. Research into legalising and regulating the sale and use of hard drugs is one possible example – can you think of others? Many a researcher will lament that their research findings are left to gather dust on the shelves of those who commissioned the research because it came up with the 'wrong' evidence.

We can see, then, that EBT comes with much baggage. Nevertheless, it is important that the spirit of evidence-based practice is not lost in all the hot air and ill-feeling about the way it is sometimes used (or not). As Tara explained in her *Unicorns* saga (▷89) notions of what constitutes evidence are not the cold and remote concerns of distant academics and researchers, but central to conscientious, committed, everyday practice.

TOUR: WHAT IS EVIDENCE OF SUCCESS?

Different views of evidence of success

We are expected to look for evidence of what works well and to use this. An approach of 'that's how we've always done it' is not good enough; we should know what evidence there is to support what we are doing. However, there are a lot of things we do not have much evidence about, and most situations are very complicated, so evidence is not simple. Taking an example from everyday life of a house extension, what might be the evidence that it was *successful*?

➢ The person living in the house might say it is a success if it gives them the extra space they had hoped for.

➢ The person owning the house might think it is a success if was built on time and within the agreed price and that it increased the house's value.

➢ The builder might judge it a success if it makes a profit.

➢ The architects might see success if their plans have been followed exactly.

➢ The local planning office might judge it a success if the extension meets all the regulations and planning laws.

➢ Neighbours might see success in an extension that doesn't shade their garden.

➢ People across the street might see success in an extension that is in keeping with the neighbourhood.

➢ Environmentalists would see success in an extension built with sustainable materials and a low carbon footprint.

➢ Family and friends might judge it a success if it gives them a comfortable spare room in which to stay when they come to visit.

(⌂3)

Practice methods

One of the tensions between theory and practice is the distinction between the essentially systematic nature of theory and what is sometimes called the *messiness* of practice. This tension is real, but it should not be used as an excuse to throw one's arms up in the air at the seeming impossibility of mapping systematic practice.

A key mechanism by which theory and practice can be successfully harnessed and integrated is through the knowledge and use of a practice method. Practice methods are ways of working with people which follow a recognisable course, but which should also be responsive to individuals and their circumstances. These are the key characteristics:

➢ A practice method is a way of working which Is *systematic.*
➢ It is based on a particular body of knowledge, perhaps organized into a *theory*.
➢ It is *tested* in practice and *researched*, so that it can be replicated, and refined.
➢ It is able to *adapt* to individual and particular circumstances without losing its basic structure.
➢ It is explicit about its *value base*.
➢ It has a *practice technology*, which guides how you use it in practice. There might be a number of associated *techniques* (e.g. the *task planning and implementation sequence* (TPIS) in task-centred practice; *paradoxical injunction* in family counselling).

One 'family' of practice methods is based around problem solving. Solution-focused, task-centred, cognitive behavioural and neuro-linguistic programming are examples of practice methods in this grouping. They each have recognised patterns of practice which are capable of being replicated in very different circumstances, but can also adapt so as to respond to variations in individual circumstances. They focus on the potential for change, and a belief based on evidence that change comes about through doing and/or rethinking. The evidence base is developed because there are sufficient examples of the methods being replicated and evaluated in practice. In some cases this leads to a systematic directory of the practice method's scope and use (☞2).

Groupwork, too, is a practice method, though it is also a *context* for practice; for example, cognitive behavioural methods can be used one-to-one or in groups. Group-based cognitive behavioural work would require an understanding of group theory in addition to cognitive behavioural theory (☙3).

There is no expectation that you should develop expertise in a wide range of practice methods; in the time available on placements this would be unreasonable. The good news is that familiarity with one practice method will give you confidence in the *notion* of a practice method, how it can work and what makes it a practice method as opposed to a series of *ad hoc* activities. If you can become expert in just one practice method you will have strengthened your professionalism immeasurably.

OTHER SOURCES

It can be hard to show students the difference between just 'doing tasks' (how could you not 'do tasks'?!) and *task-centred social work* as an actual practice method. We only have a day on task-centred in the methods course, so it's on placement that students have the chance to really get to grips with any particular method. Shama was very interested in task-centred social work and did a lot of reading about it, but her supervisor at *Family Links* didn't know this method and didn't feel he could supervise it. In a pre-placement contact I briefly outlined the method and he felt that it would be compatible with the work they do at *Family Links*, so we agreed that I would ask a social worker in a nearby agency if she'd provide supervision specifically in this method. It's vitally important that everyone knows each other's responsibilities when you have this kind of arrangement. It worked fine and a positive side effect was that the supervisor at *Family Links* developed a strong interest in this practice method and self-taught it.

Ali Chowdrey, tutor

Procedural practice

In one sense, a method is not something which you can choose to use: whenever you work with people using social work services you are using some kind of 'method'. What differs is the extent to which the method is systematic or not, explicit or implicit, tested or untested, and so on. You have a responsibility to make your methods as open as possible to the people you use them with.

There is anecdotal evidence that systematic practice methods are not commonly practised (this is as an example of current practice wisdom, one might say). If this is the case, what are the possible consequences? In a situation where there is an absence of practice method, procedures quickly fill the void. Procedures are attractive because they offer a quick, standardised and relatively cheap way of responding to demand. You have seen the way personalised services have given way to standardised ones in telephone answering services, where touch-dial responses to a menu of questions is replacing interpersonal communication. Despite the rhetoric of customer service, few customers prefer this system, but it is undoubtedly much cheaper for the provider. In human services such as social work, the touch-dial is mirrored by tick-box assessment procedures which efficiently gather the information that an agency needs in order to make a decision rather than helping the service users to tell their story. Indeed, relational aspects of social work are often belittled by policy makers and politicians as 'tea-drinking', inefficient and time-consuming diversions from the worker's main task of gathering data for the agency.

Practice methods are important not just as a lynchpin for theory and practice, but also to put professional practice on the map. Practice methods are not anti-procedural, indeed they rigorously follow procedures; but they are professionally-derived procedures and, as such, they help to give professions such as a social work their identity. Make sure that you use your placement to get a good grounding in one practice method, whichever it might be.

Professional compass

Let us return to the *Socialworkland* analogy. We have a landscape, mapped on pages xviii–xix and in Chart 4.1, but like any mapped landscape, the reality is not nearly so easy to find your way around. We will see in the next chapter the importance of your guide, the supervisor, in introducing you to *Socialworkland*, but at this point let us consider the significance of what we might call your *professional compass*. This is how you get your bearings, how you know where you are in the greater scheme of things.

This notion of *professional compass* might not make immediate sense. The theory is that you need to develop a good sense of what is right and wrong in professional practice, as well as the evidence base that helps you decide what works and what doesn't. These notions are not straightforward and it is in the 'grey areas', the ambiguous or uncertain elements that characterise much of social work practice, that having a good compass is important. Let us take a specific example:

➢ A social worker invites a service user to pray with him/her.

Where would you situate this activity on the professional compass (Chart 4.3)? If it was highly ethical and highly effective it would be charted at A1; if highly unethical and highly ineffective it would be at F6; there are 34 other possible chartings in between. Of course, this is not meant to be a scientific process – that is the whole point of attempting to pinpoint what is, essentially, very ephemeral. However, attempting to chart this activity against its moral and practical dimensions does lead you to consider *how* you might do this, who and what might you need to help you do it, and what variables your charting might depend on.

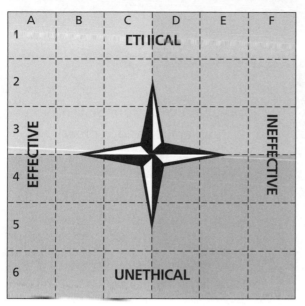

✦   *Chart 4.3: Professional compass*

We have described the charting of this scenario as an ephemeral activity, i.e. one that is hard to grasp in any concrete way; it does, nevertheless, reflect very real situations. The more oiled your professional compass, the more ready you will be to make these kinds of chartings when the time comes (▷*Professional conduct*, 135, for more examples).

Reflective practice and the competence approach

There is a lively debate in social work, and indeed in other professions, about the relationship between *the competence approach* and the idea of *critical reflective practice*. The former is illustrated by the requirement that you demonstrate your ability to perform the National Occupational Standards for social work to a required standard (▷19, ▷129). The latter finds expression in the expectation that you can relate these competences to a broader picture, one which takes account of the evidence base and the value base of social work, and that you can learn from your practice (▷*Reflection*, 73).

TOUR: DICTIONARY re-VISITED

re·flec·tion *n.*
1. Careful thought, especially the process of reconsidering previous actions, events or decisions.
2. A clear indication or the result of something.

com·pe·tence or **com·pe·ten·cy** *n.*
1. The ability to do something well or to a required standard.
2. A person's internalised knowledge of the rules of a language that enables them to speak and understand it.

See also *performance*

An example of what this means in practice is evident when we consider the *Professional compass* scenario in which a social worker invites a service user to pray with them. The social worker could perform this competently – both the invitation and the praying; however, we need critical reflective practice to know *why* and *whether* the social worker should make this invitation.

Although competence and reflective approaches are sometimes seen as polarised – opposite to one another – this is only the case if they get out of balance. Of course, social workers need to be competent at what they do; of course, they need to be able to reflect on why they are doing what they do and how it relates to the bigger picture. It is not just *what* you do, but *how* and *why* you do it that are significant. Keep this notion of a good balance in mind and talk about it with your supervisor; then, if you feel that there is an imbalance, it is easier to discuss how to re-balance it.

◁ Click to download

◁1 More information about the Peters projection
▷ www.petersmap.com

⌂2 An insight into why some consider randomised controlled trials to be
important in the health field:
▷ Sibbald, B. and Rolan, M. (1998), 'Understanding controlled trials:
why are randomised controlled trials important?' *BMJ* 1998;
316:201 (17 January) www.bmj.com/cgi/content/full/316/7126/201
(scroll down for the free access registration)

⌂3 How is the impact of service user participation measured?
▷ Doel, M., Carroll, C., Chambers, E., Cooke, J., Hollows, A., Laurie,
L., Maskrey, N. and Nancarrow, S. (2007), *Participation: Finding
Out What Difference It Makes*, SCIE Resource Guide 7, London:
Social Care Institute for Excellence (SCIE) www.scie.org.uk

📚 Books, articles, research reports

📖1 A general 'map' of social work and many of its debates:
▷ Adams, R., Dominelli, L. and Payne, M. (eds) (2002), *Social Work:
Themes, Issues and Critical Debates* (2nd edition), Basingstoke:
Palgrave/Open University.
▷ Sheldon, B. and Macdonald, G. (2008), *A Textbook of Social Work*,
London: Routledge.

📖2 An encyclopaedic presentation of the evidence for the task-centred
practice method (with a CD-version included):
▷ Reid, W.J. (2000), *The Task Planner*, New York: Columbia
University.

📖3 A general overview of groupwork theory and practice:
▷ Doel, M. (2006), *Using Groupwork*, London: Routledge/Com Care.
An overview of theory for supervisors:
▷ Lishman, J. (ed.) (2004), *Handbook of Theory for Practice Teachers
in Social Work* (2nd edition), London: Jessica Kingsley.

CHAPTER FIVE

GUIDING

Placements are guided journeys. This is to make sure that both the student's learning and the quality of the service are safeguarded and supervised. As with all guided journeys, the guide is someone who is already familiar with the terrain; in addition to knowing the lay of the land, they also need to know how to guide. Experience helps, but if the guide has not undergone training in guiding they should have access to someone who has, such as a mentor, to help them with this task. So, during the placement, think of supervision as guiding. This chapter considers the elements of good supervision, the importance of the supervisory relationship and the boundaries to that relationship. The benefits and possible difficulties of group supervision are presented.

Links

Background information about your *Fellow travellers* ▷09–11.
More explanation of terms in *Language* ▷226–8.
The following topics have strong links with the themes in this chapter:
Arrival with other students, ▷51; *Direct observation* ▷63;
Live teaching ▷64; *Journey styles* ▷55; *Two vocabularies?* ▷85;
Interpersonal problems ▷157; *Multi-site placements* ▷186;
New and experienced supervisors ▷202; *Supervisor as learner* ▷203.
Examples of placement documents are indicated by ▷**W**, and can be downloaded at: www.routledge.com/textbooks/9780415499125

Preliminaries

Before you begin the placement, take time to reflect on your experience of supervision. For students with no prior experience and for whom this is the first placement, 'supervision' might be a blank sheet. What do you *think* supervision will be like? How do you expect or want your supervisor to guide you around *Socialworkland*? Supervisors, too, should reflect on their own experience as supervisees. If you are a qualified social worker, what are your memories of being supervised as a student and what did you value most? What are your current experiences of being supervised, as an employee in the agency where the placement is set? If you are supervising as an independent practitioner, perhaps off-site, what support needs do you have and how might they be met? Bringing all of these reflections to the first supervision session is a good way to start the important dialogue about the nature of supervision and all of your mutual hopes and expectations.

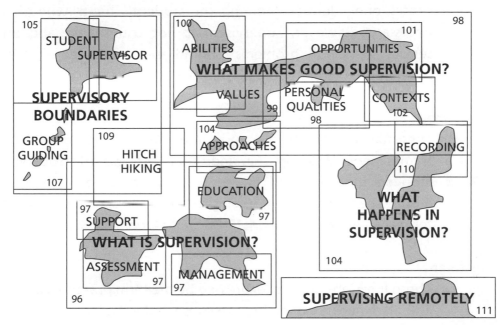

✦ *Chart 5.1: Key to guiding*

What is supervision?

In everyday English, 'supervision' refers largely to the idea of one person overseeing the work of another and having some responsibility for their work. This is true of supervision in most commercial and industrial settings. However, in professional education, and in social work education in particular, it has a more complex meaning. It incorporates four related but separate elements:

Education

E These functions are best expressed by the term *practice teacher*. The supervisor uses educational techniques to help the student's learning. Different pedagogical approaches are brought to play, including simulation and live teaching (▷*Kit*, 54–77).

Support

S These functions are best expressed by the term *mentor*. Supervision is student-centred, attending to the personal needs of the student to build the student's confidence and sense of professional identity, 'holding the student's hand' when it is necessary. However, supervision is *not* counselling and any serious personal problems should be addressed outside supervision (▷*Supervisory boundaries*, 110).

Management

M These functions are the ones most traditionally associated with the term *supervisor* as used in industrial settings. The supervisor monitors the quality of the service that the student provides, ensures agency protocols are being followed and takes responsibility for managing the placement (▷*Documentation*, 15–36).

Assessment

A These functions are best expressed by the term *practice assessor*. The placement is not a pleasure cruise, but a journey with a very explicit goal – to help the student develop social work knowledge, values and skills and to test whether the student has achieved them. The supervisor, usually in liaison with others, helps the student to gather evidence of their abilities and also makes their own judgement about the student's abilities and suitability for social work (▷*Testing*, 119–146).

What makes *good* supervision?

Good supervision is the skilful integration of all four of the functions identified above – remember it as '*ESMA*' – one in which the four elements are in balance. Good supervision arises, too, from a number of other factors. In addition to the *personal qualities of the student* (▷58), let us consider the importance of the factors outlined below.

Personal qualities of supervisors

 Supervision is an interpersonal activity; as such, the quality of the relationship between the student and supervisor is critical. Certain personal qualities in the supervisor are likely to enhance this relationship:

➢ **Commitment** – 'My supervisor made space for me and I felt she gave time to thinking about my needs as a student' (Shama Bindana).
➢ **Enthusiasm** – 'He was always interested in trying out new things and it was great to have a supervisor who was still so positive about social work' (Brenda Shapiro).
➢ **Openness** – 'We went through a bumpy time but my supervisor was always straight with me; and she was just the same with the service users – she taught me to be more trusting generally' (Tara Watson).
➢ **Supportivness** – 'I went through a really difficult time at home and it affected my placement. My supervisor didn't pry, but he was very understanding and would find time for me so I felt listened to' (Mary O'Connor).
➢ **Confidence** – 'It was important for me to feel confident in my supervisor's practice – I saw her a lot with service users and it gave me confidence seeing how good she was, and that eventually I'd be able to achieve it, too' (Nat Davies).

Values

The beliefs and values that the supervisor holds will have a bearing on how well they conduct supervision and, therefore, how this is experienced by students.

➢ **Belief in the potential of the learner** – 'I know ultimately I have to make a pass–fail judgement, but I think you need to start off with a strong belief in *potential* and it's my job to try to help each student to achieve it' (Dave Murray).
➢ **Learning as a two-way street** – 'I know it can sound a bit "pat", but I *did* learn a lot from the students and that made it a bit more of a

partnership. I asked the student to do a presentation to the team, so we all learned from her' (Cheryl Stone).

➢ **Fairness** – 'If there are disagreements I want to know that they will tell me about it so we can discuss it face to face, even if we still disagree. It's important for everyone to feel they're being treated fairly' (John Patterson).

➢ **Recognition of different needs (equal opportunities)** – 'In some ways I want the supervisor to treat me as they do everyone else, but I also want them to recognise my needs as a disabled student. It's a fine balance – the best is when it's on the table but not discussed obsessively' (Shama Bindana).

➢ **Valuing diversity and difference** – 'It's always a decision about whether to come out as gay, but I take my cue from the supervisor. If their actions and words tell me that they value difference, I will come out in my good time. But I look out for myself, too' (Nat Davies).

➢ **Commitment to involvement of users** – 'You soon pick up whether a supervisor is serious about service user involvement or whether it's going to be tokenistic. It takes real thought and planning to get proper, fair feedback about students from service users and it's a lot easier to cut corners' (Ali Chowdrey).

➢ **Integrity** – 'It's hard to define, but you quickly get a sense of whether the supervisor is "sound" – often it shows itself in humour. I like a supervisor with a sense of humour, and there's going to be some "mortuary" humour in social work, but there's a line; I can tell if it's actually disrespectful or dishonest' (Tara Watson)

(▷*Personal qualities of students*, 58).

Abilities

 What are the particular skills and abilities that a supervisor needs in order to provide good supervision? You might want to make your own list before turning to this one compiled by your fellow-travellers:

➢ **Communication skills** – 'When you look at the fact that you are teaching, assessing and supporting a student, and managing the placement all at the same time – and sometimes having to give some difficult messages, it's not hard to see why good communication skills are crucial' (Cheryl Stone).

➢ **Structuring teaching and learning** – 'It was good that my supervision sessions weren't just about checking over my cases; we'd have part of the session that was actual teaching around an agreed topic and – though it was nerve-wracking at the time – there was live teaching, too. It was very different from my experience of being supervised as a member of staff' (Brenda Shapiro).

➢ **Adaptable learning and teaching styles** – 'My supervisor could be really flexible; sometimes I just wouldn't "get" something and he'd always find another way around it to help me think outside my box' (Mary O'Connor).

➢ **Assessing standards** – 'It's not enough to have a feel for what is a good-enough standard; you need to be able to express it in concrete terms so the student knows what you're talking about and feels you're being fair – they know what you're assessing them on' (Dave Murray).

➢ **Practical knowledge base** – 'My personal experience is important for students to learn from, but my situation means that I have a lot of practical knowledge; it's given me the confidence to see myself as a supervisor as well as a service user' (Susan Chapman).

➢ **Reflection** – 'It was great when my supervisor said she was going to keep her own reflective diary during the placement, too. There's something about seeing this experienced worker still reflecting on her work, but in this case she was reflecting on the placement and her experience of being a supervisor. It was strange at first but I really learned a lot from it' (Mary O'Connor).

Opportunities

A placement is only as successful as the opportunities allow; however, some people are better at finding and making use of these opportunities. Good supervision recognises these opportunities and creates the space to develop them and use them well.

➢ **To prepare for the student** – 'We have a policy of workload relief so that supervisors have time to prepare, but the reality of this policy varies from team to team. Teams with a real commitment to student supervision make sure that the supervisor is given this space' (Viv Delaney).

➢ **For students to learn safely from planned opportunities** – 'At first I wasn't getting enough hands-on experience, but I talked about it in supervision and my supervisor and I made a detailed plan whereby I could get more directly involved without putting service users or me at risk' (Tara Watson).

➢ **For seizing the moment of unplanned opportunities** – 'I felt the placement was nicely planned but not like a straightjacket; quite a few times my supervisor would say, "Something's come up that'll interest you, do you want to come along?" It felt like he always had me in mind even when it wasn't planned and I always used to learn a lot from these spur of the moment things' (Nat Davies).

➢ **To provide a variety of learning opportunities** – 'Students get a lot out of our community group placement, there's a lot of scope; but there's some stuff we can't provide, so we have an arrangement with the local statutory services for students to spend some time with them, too' (John Patterson).

➢ **For creative practice** – 'My supervisor was good at letting me develop some really creative stuff; I was worried whether it would meet the competencies but she was able to help me see how it related to my learning objectives and to gather the evidence' (Shama Bindana).

➢ **For reflection on practice and learning** – 'I had regular supervision, an hour and a half to two hours, every week without fail, and a good part of that time was devoted to reflecting on my learning. My supervisor also made sure to protect the half-day a week for study time and work on my reflective diary and portfolio' (Brenda Shapiro).

Contexts

 Good supervision is dependent on various factors, not all of which are necessarily under the supervisor's control. Contextual factors within the supervisor's team or agency and within the social work programme as a whole can have a large bearing on the way that supervision is experienced.

- **Organisation of the practice learning** – 'We have good support from our agency partners, who keep updated intelligence about where the placements are available and any additional support that might be needed' (Sandra Townsend).
- **Clarity of aims and shared expectations** – 'We've all been involved in developing the placement protocols – the portfolio and all the documentation that goes with it – so there's a shared understanding of what placements are supposed to provide for the students' (Viv Delaney).
- **Agency commitment to practice learning** – 'Supervising students is in the job descriptions of all the qualified staff that we employ and we make sure that accredited training is available. Latest figures show that we recruit 35 per cent of our new staff through having them on placements with us, so we want them to have a good experience' (Viv Delaney).
- **Resources and rewards** – 'We have access to many resources for our teaching and I receive an honorarium when I supervise a student, but actually more important than this, you know, is that I feel that placements are valued in this agency – for instance, the director always meets all the students at the end of the placement for a debrief and we get a thank you and a digest of the students' comments' (Dave Murray).
- **University commitment to practice learning** – 'I have felt very supported by the tutor and the supervisor groups that the university organises. The three-day course was good, but as someone new to this and without a social work qualification, this network has been a life raft' (Cheryl Stone).
- **Available support systems** – 'The organisation where I was placed had a disability support group which, as a student on placement there, I was invited to join. It added a lot to my experience of the placement' (Shama Bindana).
- **Champions for practice learning** – 'There's only so much that you can do as a single supervisor, so the fact that we have a supportive practice learning manager and an agency director who takes a keen interest in students and placements is really important' (Dave Murray).
- **Stability in the working environment** – 'I was lucky – the team where I was placed was fully staffed and most had been there a while so they

knew the neighbourhood. There was a newly qualified worker who'd been on placement here last year and the agency have a protected first year, so if a vacancy came up I'd seriously want to consider it' (Tara Watson).

➤ **Positive attitudes of team members** – 'My supervisor is more of a coordinator. I mean, she gives me weekly supervision and that, but she makes sure I get to work with the rest of the team and I like that. They've all got different styles so it's interesting to have the different contacts and I always feel that if my supervisor got sick or something the rest of the team could step in' (Mary O'Connor).

Approaches

There are many ways in which styles of supervision can be typified. Below are three. Do any of them ring bells? What are the advantages and disadvantages of each of them and how, as a supervisor, would you typify your own approach? What would you *like* your approach to be?

The Modeller

'I draw upon my own experiences as a supervised student, and attempt to do (or not to do) what my supervisor did with me.'

The Aviator

'I extemporise, "winging it" and learning through trial and error.'

The Builder

'I systematically review my supervision practice, build on best practices and consciously stretch myself.'

What happens in supervision?

There is surprisingly little formal research into the fine detail of what actually goes on in social work student supervision. One small project from the early 1990s indicated the following (📖1):

Content of the supervision sessions

64 per cent of supervision time was devoted to case or work discussion. This suggests that some student supervision is not dissimilar to case-based staff supervision. Perhaps this has changed in the 15 years since this study, given the developments in training for practice teachers, but it would be interesting to replicate the study to test this one way or another.

Techniques used by practice teachers

The study codified the techniques used by the supervisors, with these results:

➢ offering opinions (34 per cent of activities)
➢ questioning (22 per cent)
➢ clarifying/summarising (17 per cent)
➢ information giving (13 per cent).

The largest grouping, offering opinions, suggests that the experience of supervision was more didactic than facilitative, though again we should remind ourselves of the small size of the study and the passing of time since it was conducted.

Frequency with which practice teachers referred to theory

The study made a specific count of the extent to which supervisors referred to theory during the observed sessions, with these results:

➢ 1.05 per cent alluded to theory.
➢ 0.35 per cent referred to it directly.

Even adding direct and tangential references together, we see that less than 2 per cent of the time in supervision was devoted to any mention of theory. That's well short of two minutes in a one and a half hour session!

As a supervisor, you could do your own local replication of this study by agreeing with the student to audiotape your supervision session and, using the codes above, review the tape to discover how often you use which techniques. Which techniques would you hope to deploy most?

Supervisory boundaries

Earlier in the chapter we considered the four major functions of supervision, one of which is support (▷ *ESMA*, 102). This is a grey area of supervision, in that it is unlikely to be specified in the Learning Agreement and it is frequently spoken of in general, vague terms. 'Support' means different things to different people (☃2).

STUDENT–SUPERVISOR BOUNDARIES

I had a lot of self-doubt in my first placement, on top of loads of demands from my family who'd always relied on me a lot but couldn't see that I needed more time for myself and resented me making my own way. I was afraid that I if I showed any weakness to my supervisor I'd be out of the placement and off the course; I also felt if I 'gave in' to my feelings then I'd just collapse altogether and never find my strength again, so I was busy trying to deny there was anything wrong, even to myself. It was a huge strain and it was blocking my learning on the placement.

I was fortunate that my supervisor picked up on all this. Right at the beginning of the placement we'd done the *Student Boundaries* exercise (▷46) and he suggested we have another look at it. When it came to the fifth question, *Would you talk about personal matters on placement?*, he looked directly at me and asked me what was wrong. He said that I shouldn't be afraid to let it out and, that way, I could at least get some help with it – and then I let it all flow. In the end I took a break from placement, got myself some help, and when I came back I was in a much better state to make a go of it. It wasn't easy – I had some catching up to do because it's hard if you slip out of synch with the course, but it was the best thing I did. My supervisor doesn't know the details of what was happening at home – he didn't need to – but he really helped me to face it.

Mary O'Connor, student

Perhaps one of the greyest areas surrounds student's personal lives. Clearly, all students have lives outside their studies and we should remind ourselves that, more often than not, these other lives are a source of strength and support; but when this is not the case, to what extent should supervisors provide support? Where does the supervisory boundary lie? A rule of thumb is that if the personal is having an adverse impact on the professional, then these issues need to be openly discussed, *but only so far as they concern the professional*. That is the important boundary: supervision is not therapy, though it may have therapeutic effects. If you need personal help and counselling, this need can be discussed in supervision (and, of course, some discussion of your personal life will have been necessary to come to this conclusion), but the service itself needs to be provided elsewhere.

Group guiding

REFLECTIONS OF A GROUP SUPERVISOR

I facilitate a group of seven social work students every two weeks for two hours. The students are all on placement in our agency and they each receive day-to-day supervision with a designated on-site supervisor.

Every session we start with a check-in, which is when everyone shares their homework (see later), then a round when each briefly shares a 'headline' – for example, a significant event or 'light-bulb' learning moment, and also one main issue they'd like to talk about. We look for common themes (never difficult to find) and then agree which topics we're going to focus on. The themes can be anything – practice dilemmas, use of supervision, a values question, risk taking, assessment problems. I'll ask one of the students who raised the issue to kick us off with something very concrete to illustrate what it's about; some find this easier than others – to be concrete – but they soon learn from one another. Sometimes we'll turn the discussion into some kind of rehearsal (I avoid the word 'role-play'!) other times we'll stay with discussion. At the end of each topic we go round and I ask each student to summarise what the discussion has meant to them and how they see it influencing their learning and practice. I will attempt to root at least one of the topics into a theoretical framework and prepare homework for the students, which usually entails them doing some problem solving and chasing up further reading. They bring their findings to the next session. Now that I have established this pattern I think the students could run it themselves. Well, that's not actually true, it does take some facilitation, but when it's working well, it's really more a question of serving the group than leading it.

I always give myself an hour after the session to do the research for the homework and email it to them all. I make some brief notes on the session, too. I'm looking to do a post-qualifying module in groupwork but haven't found one yet.

Dave Murray, supervisor

Support comes not just from your supervisor, the team and your tutor, but also from other students. This might be very informal, or via some form of electronic *social networking* (▷74). Increasingly, social work courses are also providing opportunities for group supervision. Although some of the motivation for supervision in groups is economic (six or more students are supervised in the time it would take to work with one), there are better, pedagogical reasons to promote group supervision. Dave Murray leads a regular supervision group and shares his reflections opposite; students Tara Watson and Brenda Shapiro tell their own very different stories of group supervision on page 114.

EXPERIENCES OF GROUP SUPERVISION

I enjoyed the chance to get together with the other students; we felt very supportive of each other and we learned a lot. There were six of us in the group and it was amazing how common the issues were, even though we were from very different settings and different courses. The group supervisor could make the links for us, though we got better at doing this for ourselves as time went on.

There was a rather dominant student, but the supervisor skilfully shared out the time without seeming to put him down. I liked the way she structured the session; there was like a regular pattern but it didn't feel we were being forced either. It was good to talk about some of the issues in the group with my on-site supervisor, one-to-one.

Our facilitator was very clear about how the group supervision would be assessed. Actually, you learned more about people in the group setting – I know who I would've liked as my social worker!

Tara Watson, student

Attendance wasn't bad to begin with, but soon it got so as you wouldn't know who was going to be there, which made it very disruptive. Actually, I missed a couple of times when I decided on other priorities. Also, I couldn't see the point of having people from different settings and different courses; it was hard to see what there was in common and people went off at tangents all the time.

I was the most experienced there and I just felt like I was telling everybody what to do all the time, so it didn't feel very two-way, if you know what I mean. And one person didn't seem to know what was appropriate in terms of self-disclosure, which made me feel awkward.

The group supervisor was very knowledgeable about certain things, but she tended to let people go on and most times we ran over time. I didn't get one-to-one supervision the weeks we had group supervision and I missed not having that.

Brenda Shapiro, student

↗ Count the number of times that Tara and Brenda each use 'we/us' and 'I/me'.

Also important is group support for supervisors. In the next chapter, we explore how the *Wisdom of the group* (▷137) helps Cheryl Stone to take a step back when there is much conflicting evidence. These forums can provide a sigificant opportunity for reflection; the mutual commitment that group members have towards one another means that individuals are less likely to allow the time to be 'stolen' by other activities (☙3).

Hitch-hiking

Your named guide, the work-based supervisor, practice teacher and/or practice assessor, is likely to provide the bulk of your supervision, but always be on the look-out to hitch a ride with one your colleagues. It is something to discuss with your supervisor whether this has to be formally agreed with them, or whether you have open permission to take up these opportunities as they occur.

HITCH WITHOUT A HITCH

💬

Janey, one of the workers in the team where I'm placed, is doing some really interesting work with a social worker at the local school. The social worker's using a 'cognitive counselling' method of work (☙4) and Janey said she'd phone her and ask if I could come along to meet her this afternoon. There might even be a chance for me to see the method in action if the young person agrees. My supervisor was away for two days, so I was really pleased that we had already agreed early in the placement that it would be good for me to experience other practitioners at work. Some of these were arranged by my supervisor, but she'd said that it was fine for me to 'hitch a ride' if ever the opportunity came up. She just wanted me to write about it afterwards in my reflective log so that we could talk together about my learning from it in the next supervision session. She said, 'You can enjoy it, but it isn't a joy ride!'

Nat Davies, student

Recording supervision

Many programmes or agencies have developed their own templates or forms for recording supervision. Although it is helpful when someone else has done the preparation (by making the form), it is also useful to have gone through the thought processes yourself. For example, who should be responsible for taking notes of supervision sessions – the student, the supervisor, both, or alternating? What is the purpose of the supervision notes? Will they be included in the final documentation that the student presents as evidence? Clearly, notes made in supervision might take on a different aspect if they are later brought into play because of difficulties in the placement (▷*Keeping a log*, 164).

In general, both student and supervisor should prepare the agenda for each supervision session, preferably in advance so that any other kinds of preparation (reading file records, etc.) can be completed as needed. It is no bad thing to share responsibility for documenting the supervision session, perhaps with the supervisor taking notes the first few times to set the tone. Notes should usually be succinct and act as an aide-memoire of what was discussed and agreed in the session. For an example of supervision notes ▷*Writing up*, 141.

REFLECTIONS ON SUPERVISION

I'd ask my student about how she was getting on with her placement diary, the reflective journal, and she kept shying away from talking about it. When you're a student is the time to really get to grips with this because it has to come 'naturally' when you're in full-time work and busy with a full caseload, when you don't get the chance to practise it. Actually, I found that when I did my 'Enabling learning' module, this was the first real attempt I had made to do this – be reflective – and my reflections on the supervision I was giving were really helpful. I have learned that with any future students I'll make sure that the placement diary is a definite requirement because I wasn't sure what my grounds were in pushing it.

Cheryl Stone, supervisor

Supervisors working remotely

Increasingly there are pressures for social workers to work from home, sometimes referred to as *working remotely*. As well as the possible implications for the development of teamwork, this practice would also have an impact on the student experience (⊠1).

⊠ Click to download

⊠1 A study on the impact of supervisors working remotely:
   ▷ heather@hpritchardconsultancy.co.uk

≋ Books, articles, research reports

≋1 A research study into the fine detail of student supervision in social work:
   ▷ Brodie, I. (1993), 'Teaching from practice in social work education: a study of the content of supervision sessions', *Issues in Social Work Education*, 13:2 pp71–91.

≋2 A research study into the way practitioners define their boundaries with people who use social services:
   ▷ Jayarantne, S., Croxton, T. and Mattison, D. (1997), 'Social work professional standards: an exploratory study', *Social Work*, 42:2 pp187–98.

≋3 A useful guide to group supervision:
   ▷ Atherton, S. (2006) *Putting Group Learning into Practice*, West Midlands Learning Resource Network/Skills for Care.
   Also:
   ▷ Bogo, M., Globerman, J. and Sussman, T. (2004), 'The field instructor as a group worker: managing trust in group supervision', *Journal of Social Work Education*, 40:1, pp13–26.

≋4 AERO (Aspirations, Encouragement, Realism, Openness) is a method of school social work, but transferable to other settings:
   ▷ Bramble, R. (2008) *Aspirations, Encouragement, Realism and Openness: A Guide to Help Increase Children's happiness and Potential inside and outside Schools*, UK: Bramble Jordan Publishing.

📚5 Useful texts about supervision practices and placement learning and teaching:

▷ Beverley, A. and Worsley, A. (2007), *Learning and Teaching in Social Work Practice*, Basingstoke: Palgrave Macmillan.

▷ Brown, A. and Bourne, I. (1996) *The Social Work Supervisor*, Buckingham: Open University Press.

▷ Caspi, J. and Reid, W.J. (2002) *Educational Supervision in Social Work: A Task-centered Model for Field Instruction and Staff Development*, New York: Columbia University Press.

▷ Hawkins, P. and Shohet, R. (2007), *Supervision in the Helping Professions* (3rd edition), Berkshire: McGraw-Hill.

▷ Healey, J. and Spencer, M. (2007), *Surviving Your Placement in Health and Social Care: A student handbook*, Buckingham: Open University Press.

▷ Lawson, H. (ed.) (1998) *Practice Teaching: Changing Social Work*, London: Jessica Kingsley.

▷ Parker J. (2005), *Effective Practice Learning in Social Work*, Exeter: Learning Matters.

▷ Pritchard, J. (ed.) (1994), *Good Practice in Supervision: Statutory and Voluntary Organisations*, London: Jessica Kingsley.

▷ Rogers, J. (2001), *Adults Learning* (4th edition), Berkshire: Open University Press.

▷ Rogers, A. (2003), *What is the Difference? A New Critique of Adult Learning and Teaching*, Leicester: National Institute of Adult Continuing Education (NIACE).

▷ Thompson N., Osada M. and Anderson B. (1994), *Practice Teaching in Social Work* (2nd edition), Birmingham: PEPAR Publications.

▷ Walker, J., Crawford, K. and Parker, J. (2008), *Practice Education in Social Work: A Handbook for Practice Teachers, Assessors and Educators*, Exeter: Learning Matters.

CHAPTER SIX

TESTING

On the placement journey your guide is responsible not just for helping to find opportunities for learning, but also for testing your progress. Although you are a student, and therefore not expected to know the landscape like your supervisor, there are standards that you are expected to achieve. These standards apply to your knowledge of the social work landscape and your ability to interact with it. Your conduct during the journey is part of that assessment, it must conform to the professional code of practice and be consistent with social work values. There will be formal and informal assessments of your progress and a judgement made as to whether it is good enough. You will need to learn how to collect evidence and to present it for others, so they can come to a fair and informed judgement. This process can be challenging and this chapter will help all involved to get the best out of it.

Links

Background information about your *Fellow travellers* ▷09–11.
More explanation of terms in *Language* ▷226–8.
The following topics have strong links with the themes in this chapter:
National occupational standards ▷19; *Practice portfolio* ▷28; *Direct observation* ▷63; *Reported practice* ▷60; *The going gets tough* ▷147–70; *Feedback, audit and monitoring* ▷208; ▷*Service user feedback* ▷212.
Examples of placement documents are indicated by ▷**W**, and can be downloaded at: www.routledge.com/textbooks/9780415499125

Preliminaries

As we discovered in the previous chapter, the placement is a site for teaching and learning about practice. It is also the place where this learning and practice is assessed. You need to be thoroughly familiar with the documentation that will be used to examine your work, usually a *portfolio* (▷28,▷**W**); also, you need to know the criteria that will be used to judge your ability, primarily the *occupational standards* (▷19); and to be aware of the *protocols* if your practice is considered to be marginal or failing (▷147–70).

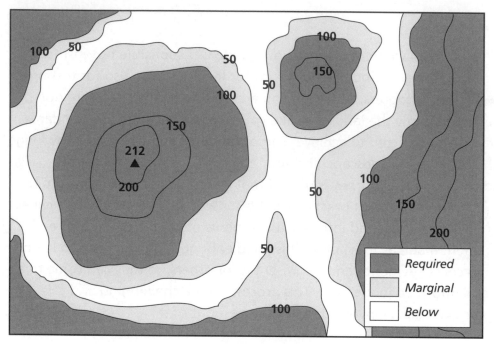

✦ *Chart 6.1: Relief map of Socialworkland*

Mindset

The idea and reality of testing are not neutral; indeed, the word 'testing' is used deliberately in this guide to help expose the feelings and anxieties that this activity provokes. Whatever the test – a written examination from your school days, an oral exam for a foreign language, the practical part of a driving test – it involves a situation where you are put on the spot and a judgement is being made about you and your abilities. Even though the placement test is called 'assessment' and is ongoing rather than a one-off test done against the clock, your response is likely to be governed by your past experiences and reactions to tests; it is important that you are honest with yourself and others about your feelings and that you cultivate an outlook that is as positive as possible towards the assessment aspects of the placement. Energies spent trying to cover up anxieties, or second-guess the supervisor, or delay testing by avoiding presenting evidence, are energies wasted; they would be better spent confronting the fears and anxieties themselves.

Supervisors, too, should consider their feelings about being the one who tests. It is a responsible role and one that can evoke feelings of anxiety about the reliability of their judgement and the likely difficulties if they decide to question the student's abilities or conduct. As a supervisor, you should make sure that you have adequate support, either from an individual mentor and/or a supervisors' support group (▷*Wisdom of the group*, 137). If you are off-site, you will need to consider the challenges of accurately accessing the student's practice through *direct observation* and *live teaching*, so that you are not overly dependent on inferences made from the student's *reported practice* (▷60).

Pre-test

Some placements may have formal screening arrangements. On the one hand these are opportunities for the placement provider and the student to find out more about each other and to see whether there is likely to be a fit; on the other hand, they are a kind of pre-test, rather like the way you test a microphone to see if it's going to work OK later.

In *Testing, testing* (▷122), there is no doubting that the door that Nat 1 has chosen to walk through leads to a pass, whereas Nat 2's choice results in a fail. The consequences in this case are restricted merely to the question of access to this particular placement (granted or denied), but the lessons of this experience are much more wide-ranging. For all the conversational tone that developed in Nat 1's case, this *is* a test and, already, you can see that there is much to be learned from failing a test as well as passing it – if you are receptive to these lessons. Nat 2, you might feel, is not inclined to see any learning from his experience: why do you think this is and how could this be changed? Are there circumstances in which you might find it hard to see, accept or act on lessons from difficult experiences?

DOOR 1   TESTING, TESTING …   DOOR 2

I hadn't known quite what to expect even though they'd said in the email that a panel of self-advocates would be making the decision about whether the placement would go ahead with me. As it turned out it gave me a good feel for the place and I guess they were able to make their mind up about me, too. It felt right that they were deciding.

I've not got any experience of working with people with learning difficulties but I took my cue from the panel and answered their questions as best I could. It turned into more of a conversation and the more I heard about what they did the more interested I became – the organisation covers employment, housing, education, all sorts. I asked about what they saw a student adding to the life of the place and also how they felt they could help my learning. I was really glad when they offered me a placement.

Nat Davies, student

I was a bit late because I hadn't realised how far it was and it threw me to discover there was a group of the learning disabled about to interview me to see if I was suitable for the placement, which struck me as a bit PC if I'm honest. I didn't know whether they would understand everything I said, so I tried to keep it as simple as I could without being patronising. Fortunately the supervisor was also on the panel – she's a qualified social worker – and I thought she'd be able to explain things if necessary. Turns out I wasn't offered a placement. They said they thought it wouldn't be a good 'fit' and when I queried this they said they felt I talked to Sal (that's the social worker) rather than them, which is completely wrong, but probably shows how it would have been like walking on eggshells, so it's a bit of a relief if I'm honest.

Nat Davies, student

Taking snapshots

Tourists like to have their photographs taken in front of famous landmarks like the Taj Mahal. Perhaps part of the motivation is it proves they were there, as well as the memories it will provide. As you make your progress through *Socialworkland*, you will need to think about how to take 'snapshots' of your experiences. These, too, are evidence of your journey. Of course, photographs are relatively easy to compose and take; it is more of a challenge to think about how learning and practice can be captured in this way. A *placement diary* or log (▷33) is one method, especially if you can begin cataloguing your snapshots to represent the outcomes that are detailed in your *Learning Agreement* which, in turn, will be related to the *National Occupational Standards* (▷19). At first this might feel rather awkward and artificial, but with the guidance of your supervisor you will soon become familiar with the best way to take these snapshots and to catalogue them so they can be presented in your final album, the *practice portfolio* (▷28).

Assessment

Assessment is the process whereby a judgement is made about the quality and standard of your learning and practice. To make this process a fair one, it is important to know what criteria will be used to test your learning and practice. *Criteria* are the factors that specify what you will be assessed on and how you will be assessed. For example, for the practical part of the driving test, you know before taking the test what good driving is considered to be (through the *Highway Code*, for example); you know what driving abilities will be tested (as indicated by the examiner's mark list) and how they will be tested (through a demonstration of your practical abilities). At the end of the test you have a mark card which shows how you did in respect of each of the criteria. If you fail you know precisely why.

One of the most important aspects of a test is knowing what *evidence* is being looked for. There are two kinds of evidence – one is the negative kind that shows the absence of poor practice (in the driving test, for example, that you have not mounted the curb; you have not gone through a red light); the other is the positive demonstration of good practice (that you signalled clearly an intention to pull out; that you reverse-parked the car safely and accurately). In social work there has been a movement from a reliance on negative evidence (i.e. you didn't demonstrate poor practice) to a strong emphasis on positive evidence (i.e. you present evidence of good enough practice).

You will come across the term *indicators*. These are milestones along your placement journey that indicate the extent of your progress. Being able to engage the car in reverse gear and control it in reverse motion in a straight line is an indicator of your progress to achieving the more complex skill of reversing around a corner, for instance. In social work testing there are attempts to provide bullet point lists of *indicators*, but it is probably more meaningful when you and your supervisor are able to recognise indicators *in the context* of your own learning and practice. Often this will be a retrospective activity, perhaps through reflection in supervision, when an interaction is recognised as indicating your progress towards one of the larger learning objectives (▷ *You need three legs for a stool*, 132) for an example of how you can develop your own criteria for good practice with the help of your supervisor.

We have used the driving test as an example of testing. Of course, there are significant differences between the driving test and social work assessment, not least the complexity of an interpersonal process compared with a largely mechanical one. Also, in social work testing, your *learning* is being assessed as well as your practice. This sometimes takes a back seat, but demonstrating your learning is central to the way in which you collect evidence about your reflections. It means that even work that does not provide a successful outcome can still be an indicator of successful learning (▷ *Competence and reflective practice*, 97, and ▷ *Testing values*, 136).

When you have been on placement a few weeks, consider four scenarios from the placement setting (hypothetical if needs be, but realistic) that could illustrate the four quadrants in Chart 6.2:

- ➢ somewhere in quadrant A1–C3 (successful learning and successful practice)
- ➢ somewhere in quadrant F1–D3 (successful learning but unsuccessful practice)
- ➢ somewhere in quadrant A6–C4 (successful practice but unsuccessful learning)
- ➢ somewhere in quadrant F6–D4 (unsuccessful practice and unsuccessful learning).

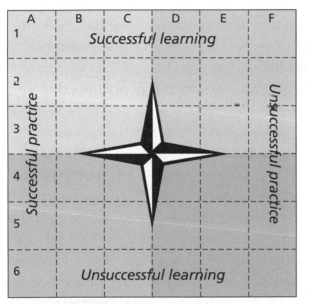

✦ *Chart 6.2: Successful and unsuccessful learning and practice*

A note on the term 'assessment'
'Assessment' is used frequently in social work to describe activities with service users, with unfortunate overtones of testing and 'doing to' rather than 'doing with'. The term is so deeply embedded in policy, legislative and organisational language that it is not possible to eradicate it.

What is evidence?

 When anthropologists want evidence of past civilisations they search for the footprint that these peoples left behind; sometimes this is literally a footprint fossilised in rock.

Think of evidence as your *personal footprint*, the mark that you make on the placement. An actual footprint is visible and tangible, but we are using the word in a metaphorical sense. So, how can you make this footprint visible and communicate it to those who will need to make a judgement about whether the evidence is sufficient?

Let us consider four different sources of evidence.

Experience

 'Seeing is believing' is the essence of experiential evidence, though the experience does not rely solely on the one sense of sight, of course. Experiential evidence lies behind the requirement for direct observation of your practice, so that the people making this judgement have unmediated access to your work. It would be folly to assess a pianist on her description of how she plays without actually listening to her playing, and the same is true of social work 'playing'. Although the evidence of our senses is very strong, we also need to be aware that we interpret our experiences and that we have a considerable capacity to read this experience selectively (▷*Self-awareness*, 62). We can imagine that the experiences of the various players in *Testing, testing ...* (▷122) were at considerable odds with one another. So, though we can see a fossilised footprint, it might not be recognised for what it is and we might rely on an interpretation of this experience in order to fully understand its significance.

Anecdote

 Though not admissible in court, 'hearsay' or retold experience can nevertheless be a source of useful evidence. Sometimes, when this is collected more systematically over time and transmitted within a profession, it is referred to as *practice wisdom*. This form of evidence is important if only because it seems to have a disproportionately large impact on what professionals actually *do* – though that assertion is itself an example of practice wisdom! Building on accumulated experiences, this kind of evidence is likely to be highly practical for immediate use. However, it might rest on just a few high-profile examples rather than a large number of run-of-the-mill cases, and it is likely to consolidate and perpetuate existing practices (good or bad) rather than scrutinise them robustly.

Portfolio

 Although you may start out feeling perplexed as to what can count as evidence, the irony is that the problem is not finding evidence – it is all around you – but in deciding how and what to *sample*. It is the sifting of evidence that provides the challenge. The result is that your abilities to recognise and collect evidence are just about as important as your ability to practise. It might feel, then, that students who can write well are advantaged over those who cannot. There is truth in this, but the ability to select representative evidence and make judgements on the basis of this is an important social work skill, so the compilation of a portfolio tests you on something that is meaningful to your future practice, not just for the sake of the current assessment. The portfolio, or its equivalent, is the way you communicate your abilities to people who have not had the opportunity to experience your practice directly. For the pianist the equivalent would be a recording of their performance. In social work you are also expected to show how you have *reflected* on your performance.

Research

Research evidence is gathered in a systematic fashion and tested rigorously. For some, 'rigour' means nothing short of a randomised controlled trial (RCT, ▷*Pet Theories* 87) in which the environment is controlled to isolate one factor to test whether it has made a difference. This is easier to do with a pill than it is with social experience, which is why most social work researchers are satisfied with evidence that falls short of this rigour. Evidence from formal research has usually been tested in the way that practice wisdom has not, but it is not always presented in ways that can be readily used in daily practice. It is important that your own evidence is presented in the context of the relevant research evidence so that you can contextualise it and demonstrate your knowledge of the relevant research and theoretical frameworks.

Finally, be aware that the idea of 'evidence' is not straightforward. In the wider world of *evidence-based practice* (▷90) the question is often asked *whose evidence?* Are some sources of evidence given more weight than others and if so, what are the consequences of this?

BECOMING EVIDENT

Although you hear the word evidence all the time, in crime dramas and such, it was a real blank when it came to my placement. I talked with my supervisor about this and she took me with her to visit an older person she was working with, then we came straight back to the office, got some flipchart paper and did a 'quick-think' of what had gone on and how it related to as many of the units (in the National Occupational Standards) as possible. Then we focused down on just one of them, *Unit 2* ($\triangleright$20). My supervisor made each of the four elements in Unit 2 into just a plain English question which she asked me to answer:

2.1   Did we inform Mrs Ansell about our own and the organisation's duties and responsibilities; and if so, how?
2.2   How did we work together with Mrs Ansell to identify, gather, analyse and understand information?
2.3   How did we enable Mrs Ansell to analyse, identify, clarify and express her strengths, expectations and limitations?
2.4   How do we help Mrs Ansell to assess and make informed decisions about her needs, circumstances, risks, preferred options and resources?

Because we had the actual example of the visit with Mrs Ansell, and it was so recent in my memory, it was really easy to answer these questions. And the quick-think made me see how much material – evidence – you can get from just an hour. But the biggest lesson was to write things down as soon as possible afterwards. Now I keep a notebook on me, it's got all the key roles and units and I always save a good 15 minutes between appointments so I can make some fast notes – another tip from my supervisor. I'm so glad we did this early on, otherwise I know I would've been really scared by this evidence thing.

Tara Watson, student

✗ Tips for recognising and collecting evidence

✗ Read and act on the *Portfolio tips* (▷30).

✗ Get to know the National Occupational Standards (NOS) so well you could answer a pub quiz question on them (sad, yes!).

✗ Turn the Standards into plain English questions like Tara's supervisor did in *Becoming evident* (▷128).

✗ Make notes soon after an event, such as a contact with a service user or a meeting, so that the experience is fresh in your mind.

✗ Make a start at categorising your notes; if you write these on Post-its you can move them around from one unit to another in your file. (Most experiences will relate to more than one unit, so you will need to decide at some point later which ones to use where, and which ones also to discard.)

✗ Gather more pieces of evidence than you will need in the end, so you can make choices about what to *sample* – a bit like taking loads of photographs and then choosing the best or most representative to go in the album.

✗ Discuss your evidence regularly with your supervisor so you know that your idea of evidence matches your supervisor's – better to learn about any differences early on.

Testing competence

You will hear much talk of *competence* but what does this word mean? (⊡1) It is generally defined as the ability to do something well or to a required standard. This raises more questions about how we decide what is 'well' and how we define 'required standard' (▷*Competence and reflection*, 97).

Competence and standard

The *National Occupational Standards* (▷19) are an attempt to answer the question of *what* the standards should be, and the indicators illustrate *how* you might know that they have been met. There is a difference between standards plural and standard singular. The standards plural are statements of the content of the activity, whilst the standard singular is the height of the bar, as it were, at which 'required' is considered to have been met.

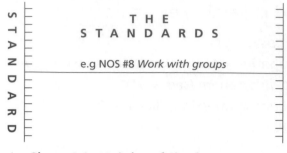

+ *Chart 6.3: Height of the bar*

Chart 6.3 shows one of the standards, National Occupational Standard 8, as a bar that is supported horizontally by two vertical poles. These vertical poles denote the idea of *standard*. In this case the NOS #8 (Work with groups) bar is perched on the seventh rung up the poles. If you can demonstrate that your learning and practice clears this level, then this might be the standard at which NOS#8 is considered competent, the *required* standard. Any practice that is only clearing the bar at the fifth or sixth rungs might be considered marginal, and anything lower than this is not competent. We can also see how the required standard, the level of the bar, could be lowered or heightened depending on whether this is a first placement or a last one, when one might have a higher standard for what is considered to be 'required' (▷*Standards*, 195).

Even when we are clear about all the terminology of testing and how the terms relate to one another, we are left with some important challenges. The first is *technical*: how do we work out what the bar looks like in practice? What is this thing called competence? We can see whether an athlete is successfully clearing an actual bar, but what does this mean for social work? The second concerns *circumstances*: should the bar be the same for everybody? What if my life circumstances make the bar more difficult to clear? The third involves *conduct*: what relevance does the manner of my competently clearing the bar have? If I push some people out of my way and squash several others in my landing, can I still be considered to have demonstrated competence because I successfully cleared the bar?

Let us explore each of these three areas in turn.

Competence and technical issues

Technical competence is measured mainly by considering output. For example, to make a judgement about your competency to write a report, we would wish to read an example of one of your reports. To assess your competency to engage with a service user, we would wish to observe you engaging with one. However, professional competence concerns itself not just with the output but also the way in which you have achieved it. You are also being assessed as a learner, because your ability as a learner indicates your capacity for professional practice in new situations, and professional practice is in many ways a succession of unique situations.

TOUR: ROASTING TIN

Whenever Sally cooked a joint of meat she cut about an inch off the end. Her daughter was puzzled and asked her why she did this, and she replied that her mother had always cut an inch off before putting it to roast. But this made Sally curious, so the next time she was with her mother she asked her why she always cut the final inch off the joint. Her mother told her that it was because *her* mother had always cut an inch off the end. Next time Sally was with her grandmother she asked about cooking a joint. Her grandmother went to the cupboard and took out a roasting tin. 'Because it's the only way I could get it to fit in this!'

So, your ability to understand and describe what constitutes a competent report – an analysis of report-writing – gives the assessor the confidence that you can produce competent reports even when the circumstances are very different. Similarly, your ability to reflect on what makes an engagement with a service user a *competent* one indicates that this example of a successful engagement can be repeated and adapted in future encounters.

YOU NEED THREE LEGS FOR A STOOL

Early on in the placement the student and I take one of their learning objectives and develop *criteria of good practice* for it. We start with an interpersonal skill such as listening. We get flip-paper and write down all the factors that we think are important; I do this as a joint exercise but some students need a bit more prompting. Then we group the factors, so that we get to about four or five. For instance, with listening, it might be:

 ➢ Don't interrupt (though we think of a few circumstances when you might).
 ➢ Maintain open body language and comfortable eye contact.
 ➢ Don't focus on what you want to say next.
 ➢ Make sure your questions build on what the person has just been saying.
 ➢ Check your understanding by summarising from time to time.

I find this exercise demystifies the idea of 'criteria'. Not all students are clear about it, but this seems to get it sorted. Then, I ask students to use these criteria as much as they can during the week – in meetings, watching a soap on the TV, when they're observing me. Just keep trying them out. At the next supervision session, they reflect on how useful the criteria were and we modify them as a result of their experiences. By now, they feel a lot more comfortable about the whole idea of criteria, good practice, indicators – all that. Next, I use these criteria to observe the student. They won't be the sole criteria I use, but skills like listening are pretty universal, so there's always an opportunity to test them. Soon after the observation we have a session for feedback on the student's competence, using the criteria. The student is now so familiar with the criteria that the assessment feels fair (they usually have a good idea themselves and, if they don't, this can be a first signal to me that there may some problems). The good thing is, once students learn this process they can reproduce it with other skills and competences. They're not just showing they can *do*, they're showing *why*; that gives me confidence they can adapt when they have to. At the same time as being assessed, they're also learning, and they are developing their practice – I always say, a stool needs three legs if it's not going to fall over!

Dave Murray, supervisor

Professional competence, as opposed just to technical competence, means that your ability is more than superficial, rote learning (2+2=4, etc,) and that you can demonstrate that you have learned the principles that underpin good practice. Fortunately, as Dave Murray makes clear in *You need three legs for a stool* (▷opposite), the process of learning can be congruent with the processes of practice and assessment, so that all three activities are integrated, not divorced from one another.

It is not possible to test everything all the time, so assessment relies on good *sampling* techniques. Dave Murray's approach in *You need three legs ...* is an example of sampling. Once he knows students are able to apply the criteria test he has taught them, he can be confident that they can reproduce this method with other aspects of their learning and practice. If he has doubts, he can ask them to reproduce the *Three legs* process with another skill area to check it out.

Competence and circumstance

When it comes to achieving the required standard (*Clearing the bar*, ▷130, chart 6.3), is it reasonable to expect everybody to achieve the same height, no matter what their circumstances? This is a complex ethical issue, but it must be made clear at the outset that the service experienced by service users must be up to standard, so it is not a question of lowering the bar. It is, however, a question of finding out what is needed to make the bar as achievable as possible, by way of individual assistance and environmental changes.

Let us take an example outside social work. We would not be happy to employ a plumber who was unable to work on any fittings below a certain height because of problems with their knees. In order to offer an effective plumbing service, it would be necessary to be able to work with fittings at any level in the house. Are there ways, then, that the person can yet fulfil their desire to be a plumber? Perhaps treatment for the knees is possible? Would additional equipment, such as a cushion, make a difference? If the plumber is working in a team, can the plumbing functions be shared so that this person can work effectively as a team member focusing on plumbing tasks that do not involve kneeling?

Returning to social work, the message is that the outcome must be a competent service, but the profession should seek ways, within reason, to ensure that individuals are given a fair opportunity to learn, practise and be assessed. Physical and intellectual disabilities are the most common circumstances to require consideration in terms of 'the bar'. A person who uses a wheelchair might be a very competent social worker despite being unable to provide a service to someone who lives on the sixth-floor of a building without wheelchair access. Dyslexia makes the processes of assimilating written material and writing slower and more difficult; in many circumstances, but not all, additional help in managing the disability can bring individuals to a point where they can achieve the bar. In all cases this will mean more effort on the part of the individual and also on the part of those who are assisting. It is a truism for the whole student group that some will need to put in more effort than others to achieve similar results.

Competence and conduct

Notions of competence are too narrow if they are restricted to technical abilities. Put simply, it is not just about whether you achieve the standards but *how*. Your conduct as a student and as a potential member of the social work profession is an important element in what is assessed. The agency in which you are placed is likely to have a code of conduct, which you should familiarise yourself with, in addition to the codes developed by the regulatory and professional bodies (⊠1). The International Association of Social Workers requires *social workers to behave in a trustworthy manner* (⊠1). Discuss with your supervisor how each of you would see 'trustworthy' in the placement setting.

TOUR: PROFESSIONAL CONDUCT

Questions for students to answer:

Should action be taken if the following information comes to light?
What action?

Questions for supervisors to answer:

Would action be taken if the following information came to light?
What action?

What codes, policies and procedures might be used and how?

Question for both of you to answer:

If *it depends*, what does it depend on?

1.   A social worker becomes engaged to a person who until two months ago was a service user of the agency that employs the social worker.
2.   A social worker overclaims mileage allowance in order to fund a group for services users.
3.   A social worker refuses to work with a same-sex couple because it contravenes the worker's religious beliefs.
4.   A social worker invites a service user to pray with him/her.
5.   A social worker masturbates a 25-year-old man who has lost use of his arms.
6.   A social worker appears on local television with a service user to publicise the service user's plight.
7.   A social worker gives advice about where a service user can purchase cannabis.
8.   A social worker becomes aware that a colleague has borrowed money from a service user.
9.   A social worker uses hypnosis with a service user.
10. A social worker invites a homeless service user back to their home to stay.
11. A social worker discusses the details of a service user (without giving the user's name), to complain about their boss to other friends on Facebook.
12. A social worker is working in a lap-dancing club as a dancer in their own time.

Try substituting social worker for 'student social worker' in each of the instances above. What, if any, difference might this make to your responses?

These scenarios were used in a research project about professional boundaries (⊠2).

One way to begin to understand what notions such as 'trustworthy' might mean in practice is to consider scenarios, sometimes called *vignettes*, of real or potential situations. One element of trustworthiness is the confidence that professionals are aware of boundary issues in their relationships with service users – the difference between a professional relationship and friendship, for example. There are also boundaries between their public and private lives which affect public confidence in the profession as a whole. Discussing the scenarios in *Professional conduct* (▷135) will help you understand more about these issues, especially that the exercise of judgement is as important as knowing what the policy document states. Codes of conduct cannot be written at the level of detail necessary to prescribe a particular action in every specific circumstance; you must develop your own ethical thinking and test it out regularly with your supervisor and, when you are qualified, with your team colleagues.

Testing values

Professional conduct is underpinned by values. For example, answering your mobile phone and making personal arrangements whilst with a service user would be considered a matter of concern in terms of your conduct – but why? Conduct is often expressed as a set of rules or procedures, but it is the values that lie behind the conduct that are important. In the example above, there would be concern that this behaviour showed a lack of respect for the service user, which violates one of social work's main values. Revisit the *Professional conduct* tour (▷135) and consider what values come into play in each scenario and how they are potentially jeopardised. By looking *beneath* the conduct you will can understand *why* issues of professional conduct are considered significant, and that codes of practice are not just about imposing inconvenient rules.

The term that is often used to describe concerns about conduct is *suitability*. Each programme has its own way of following up these concerns, and the guide will consider this in more detail later (▷ *Suitability meetings*, 166).

Testing over time

Supervisors are also 'tested' by the experience of assessing students. As we have noted earlier, it is an exciting but also challenging activity, technically and emotionally. One of the complexities of student assessment is that the picture is constantly changing, and that testing must, by necessity, take place over time. What you are expecting from the student at the beginning of the placement will be different from the end; during this time the student's practice is growing, or should be, as is your understanding and knowledge of the student. This tour, *Wisdom of the group*, explores the effects of the passage of time and the importance of strong support systems for supervisors.

TOUR: WISDOM OF THE GROUP

Supervising a placement can be a lonely experience, which is why you should join or create a support system. Meeting for an hour or so once a fortnight can provide a regular source of support and development as a supervisor. Cheryl Stone is fortunate enough to be a member of a weekly supervisors' support group, which she used to discuss the following situation with a first year student.

WEEK 1

The student arrived late on the first morning of the placement, but apologised profusely. She said she had 'domestic problems' but they had been sorted out. However, she also turned up late for a team meeting and the male receptionist said she forgot to sign a letter of appointment to see a service user. Smiling knowingly, the receptionist also said that the student had been receiving a lot of phone calls from a man.

📌 *It is nearly a week into the placement and Cheryl is going to a meeting of the supervisors' support group, at which she explains the situation. They discuss various options. What courses of action do you think they might consider and what would you advise Cheryl to do?*

WEEK 2

In response to Cheryl's concerns, the student told her about the recent death of her mother and the demands which her father had been making on her, including telephoning her at work. She apologised and said that the situation was now under control and she did not expect it to interfere with the placement.

The student's time-keeping improved, but just yesterday morning she did not come into the office and the receptionist was unable to say when she was expected back. Cheryl thought he muttered something about 'not doing any more covering up for that student of yours' and 'her off-hand attitude', but he wouldn't elaborate when Cheryl pressed him.

One of Cheryl's colleagues mentioned how useful the student's ideas had been at a planning meeting for a group of isolated women with mental health problems. During the week, Cheryl observed the student conducting an office interview and was impressed by her ability to engage with the service user and to structure the interview.

Just as Cheryl was setting off for the supervisor group, another colleague caught her quickly (Cheryl had been off sick for a few days and the colleague had not been able to speak with her before). He told Cheryl that he had invited the student as an observer to a case discussion in another agency and the student had been late and unapologetic. Cheryl's colleague was also concerned that the student had 'aggressively' taken up an issue about confidentiality with the person who was chairing the case discussion, even though the understanding had been that the student was meant to be there as an observer.

🚗 *Cheryl discussed these latest developments at the supervisors' support group. What courses of action do you think they might consider? What course would you advise Cheryl to take?*

WEEK 3

The student told Cheryl that she is allowed half a day a week study time ('it's in the Learning Agreement'), which accounted for her absence from the office that morning. She had assumed it was Cheryl's responsibility to tell the receptionist but was sorry if there was a misunderstanding. She thought the receptionist was feeling rebuffed because he'd made a pass at her which she ignored. The student was adamant that she did apologise for lateness at the case discussion (her bus hadn't turned up so she had to wait for the next one) and she couldn't understand why the colleague reported her as being unapologetic, unless he hadn't heard her because she was flustered. Also, they had just been doing ethics in college and she felt that the chair of the case discussion had breached some important issues of confidentiality. The student had felt compelled to raise them when it was clear that no one else was going to.

The colleague who is facilitating the women's group asked Cheryl if the student could join as one of the co-leaders, because 'she's got such a lot to contribute and she worked exceptionally well with the women when she was a helper on an recent outing.' Cheryl works on a individual basis with Sheila, one of the women in the group and during a recent session Sheila had nothing but praise for the student. 'She's really giving me confidence to come off my medication, too. I've always wanted to do this and now I have someone who really believes in me,' says Sheila.

At the end of the most recent supervision session with the student, Cheryl was just about to leave to get to her next appointment (the supervisors' support group as it happens) when the student told her that the tutor would be in touch to discuss the implications of a possible accusation of plagiarism in one of her essays, the one on ethics. The student says this is untrue, but she may have used some of the notes she took from her reading and transcribed them into the essay without realizing they were in fact direct quotes. She concludes, 'if it is a mistake, I guess I'll have to rewrite the essay.'

📖 *Cheryl raised the latest developments at the supervisors' support group. What courses of action might they consider? What course would you advise Cheryl to take?*

WEEK 4

At the start of the student's fourth week, if you were to make an *interim assessment* of her strengths and weaknesses, what would these be? What difference do you think the supervisors' group has made to the quality of the supervision that Cheryl is able to give?

From what you know of the *fellow-travelling students* (▷09–11), how might the recommended courses of action differ from one student to another?

Here and there

Chart 6.1, the *Relief map of Socialworkland* (▷120) is a graphic way of illustrating the notion of standards – required standard and below standard. However, the areas that can cause the most angst are the marginal ones. In these territories a small movement in one direction or the other has immense repercussions and, because testing is not an exact science, the picture can look different from one day to the next. Furthermore, the same student can be achieving the required standard for some aspects of the practice yet failing in others.

As *Wisdom of the group* demonstrates, it is important that 'readings' are taken over time, to see what changes (if any) can be spotted and also to achieve a more complete picture of the student's practice. It is also important not to confuse marginal practice as *the sum of some good and some poor practice*, a kind of mathematical average. It is possible for students to achieve required standards for some learning objectives and to be failing in others, and this should not be read as a composite 'marginal'. It is important to be specific about what the strengths and the weaknesses are. Can the strengths be harnessed to develop weaker areas? What opportunities are there to spend more time on those areas that are not considered competent, perhaps by extending the placement? We will look in more detail at options for when the going gets tough in the next chapter.

Writing up

Earlier in this chapter the photograph album was suggested as a metaphor to think about how the experiences of journeying through *Socialworkland* are recorded – sampling from many snapshots, cataloguing these and commenting on them. Supervisors are also taking their own snaps of the student's journey and providing a commentary on the pictures that the student presents.

We have emphasised that testing is a continuous process throughout the placement rather than a single event. As such, the gathering of assessment materials is also a continuous process; each supervision session is an opportunity to check on 'the album' to see whether there are sufficient materials being collected, assess whether they are appropriate to the learning objectives and establish a view of their quality. The supervision sessions themselves need to be recorded succinctly. Often a template can be used (▷**W**) and a small sample of these should be included in the final assessment documentation (also ▷*Recording supervision*, 116).

Templates are also useful to record experiences such as the *direct observation* of practice (▷63; ▷**W**), though it is important not to treat templates as tick-boxes and to allow time and space to individualise each one. Descriptions of what happened should be succinct, allowing more space to be devoted to comment, evaluation and any actions suggested from the experience. The advice is always to diary-in time to write up the record immediately after a planned event such as a direct observation, so that the recording is part of the event and not an afterthought. In most cases it is useful to have the comments of the observed and the observer, each written independently so that they can be shared, perhaps at a later date such as the next supervision session. The direct observation records are then available for the final assessment documentation.

The final assessment report should follow the particular guidance provided by the social work programme; for an example of such a template and a completed report ▷**W** (and ask your programme if they have exemplars of completed portfolios and reports for you to peruse). As a supervisor, you will find that familiarity with the pro-formas will make this task easier, but it is always important to remember that for the student this is always only the first, second or at the very most third time they have done it and your guidance is important. Most of the assessment documentation should have been gathered gradually as the placement has been progressing, so your job – as student or supervisor – towards the end of the placement is more to review and edit the materials, with just the final report or commentary to complete. The editing role is important because there will be materials to include from service users and colleagues (▷*Service user feedback*, 212), and there needs to be sufficient time to comment on these in the portfolio and the final report. Unless there have been some unexpected events in the last weeks and days of the placement, there should be nothing in the final reports that has not already been discussed and explored together.

If difficulties have been noted during the placement, a more detailed record of events will be necessary to provide evidence of concerns (▷*Keeping a log*, 164).

'On-site' and 'off-site' supervisors

If there is both an on-site and an off-site supervisor (sometimes called, respectively, work-based supervisor and practice teacher or practice assessor), it is crucial that there is good communication between them throughout the placement and especially when compiling the final documentation. The roles and responsibilities of on-site and off-site supervisors should be made clear in the *Service Agreement* (▷27), which might be incorporated into the *Learning Agreement* (▷24). Examples of supervision session notes from both supervisors should be included in the final documentation and it should be clear from the beginning of your placement what part each will play in the writing of the final report. Off-site supervisors are often required because the on-site person is not a qualified social worker, and in these circumstances the off-site supervisor will have responsibility for 'signing off' the report (that is, making the final recommendation). The on-site supervisor might provide the main first draft of the report and much of the day-to-day evidence of your practice, with the off-site supervisor giving an overview and perhaps focusing more on your learning and abilities to relate the daily experience to social work theory.

Overall, when reading the assessment materials, it should always be clear whose work is being presented at any time. If there are differences of opinion between on-site and off-site supervisors these should be apparent *before* the final reports are due so that appropriate meetings can be held with the tutor to discuss differences and agree a course of action.

Practice panels

You might wonder what happens to your portfolio and reports once they are completed and handed to the university or college. Every course has its own protocols, but they usually follow a similar path. Your tutor will read the documentation and might want to make contact if there are any specific issues, if only to enquire after a part of the documentation that might be missing or is obscure. Tutors should also at some stage write to or email the supervisors to thank them for all their work, though this is more likely to follow the meeting of the Examination Board (see later).

Social work courses have a panel or board composed of experienced supervisors, often including service users and carers, whose role it is to review the placement documentation. Often called Practice Assessment Panels, these meetings usually take a sample of documents and read them with an eye to consistency and quality; in other words, they are not necessarily marking individual portfolios, rather they are checking to see that the way work has been assessed is fair and compares across the programme. The panel agrees an annual report about the provision of practice learning on the course. This will concern itself with placement quality and also with issues like *progression*, which refers to the percentage of students who are successfully completing the course (⊠3).

DIPSTICK

I'm a member of the Practice Assessment Panel and, though it's hard work, I enjoy it and I think it's a very valuable thing to do. I think of it as a kind of 'dipstick' into the programme, testing what's coming out of it. I read about three or four portfolios and most times it's fine. One time I wasn't so sure – I won't go into the details but I was worried about what one of the students had described in their case study and it didn't seem to be picked up by the supervisor. Anyway, the tutor followed it through and asked the student and the supervisor for some more detail and context, which helped to clarify what had actually happened. The tutor said she was glad that I had picked up on it, because the student had a tendency to skate over detail and that had led to some other misunderstandings, too, so I felt I'd been useful and the student had learned the importance of presenting their evidence carefully. I enjoy meeting the other supervisors – they call them practice assessors – because it helps me think about my own supervision practices when students come to our project.

John Patterson, service user provider

Given the wide variety of practice sites and the varying experience of supervisors, quality control can be a challenge (▷*Feedback, audit and monitoring*, 208). If one of the panel readers has concerns about a particular portfolio or report, this will be read by a second member and if concerns remain, the external examiner will be asked for an opinion. The external examiner is someone who is independent from the programme, usually an experienced academic, or occasionally an independent practitioner, appointed by the university to review students' essays, assignments and portfolios. This process is called *moderation*. Like the panel, the examiner takes a sample of work that represents the whole range of quality (and they will read all work that is deemed to have failed) to consider whether academic marks and placement decisions are fair and consistent, both across the programme and between this programme and others. External examiners write an annual report about the programme and, like the practice panel's reports, these are public documents.

The comments of the Assessment Panel and the external examiner are compiled in order that a recommendation can be made to the Examination Board. The Board is constituted by the university or college and has the authority to make the final decisions. Recommendations arising from other meetings, such as *Suitability meetings* (▷166), also come to the Board for a final decision. In most cases, the Examination Board upholds the recommendations made to it, but it does have the power to overturn these and occasionally this will happen, though reasons must be given.

Appeals against decisions of the Exam Board are possible, but it is important to read the protocols for your own programme because these vary from one course to another.

◪ Click to download

◪1 Website addresses for professional codes of practice ▷53 ◪4
   The International Association of Social Workers ▷www.iaasw.org
◪2 This tour is taken from a research report on professional boundaries
   ▷ www.gscc.org.uk
◪3 The General Social Care Council publishes reports about progression
   amongst different groups of students:
   ▷ http://www.gscc.org.uk/NR/rdonlyres/31BF4B30-A92D-4195-9A1D-
   F06F4373AFCF/0/Diversityandprogressioninsocialworkeducation
   updatereportApril2008doc.pdf
   Additional research:
   ▷ http://www.gscc.org.uk/NR/rdonlyres/E4482365-4F9F-46F0-9238-
   A030302E0ED7/0/Progression_analysis_FT_UG_0305__Executive_
   Summary.pdf

📚 Books, articles, research reports

📚1 To explore issues of assessment further:
▷ Lefrevre, M. (2005), 'Facilitating practice learning and assessment: the influence of relationship', *Social Work Education,* 24:5, pp565–83.
▷ Parker J. (2005), *Effective Practice Learning in Social Work*, Exeter: Learning Matters.
▷ Shardlow, S.M. and Doel, M. (1996), *Practice Learning and Teaching,* Basingstoke: Macmillan.
▷ Yorke, M. (2005) 'Issues in the assessment of practice-based professional learning', a report for the practice-based professional learning CETL, Open University.

📚2 To explore issues of competence further:
▷ Fletcher, S. (1992), *Competence-Based Assessment Techniques,* London: Kogan Page.
▷ O'Hagan, K. (2007), *Competence in Social Work Practice: A Practical Guide for Students and Professionals* (2nd edition), London: Jessica Kingsley.

📚3 More on assessing work-based learning for social work
▷ Williams, S. and Rutter, L. (2007), *Enabling and Assessing Work-Based Learning for Social Work: Supporting the Development of Professional Practice*, Learn to Care Publication 10. Birmingham: Learn to Care. www.learntocare.org.uk.

CHAPTER SEVEN

THE GOING GETS TOUGH

When you prepare for a trip it is a good idea to pack for all kinds of weather. Perhaps you also take out insurance to cover the possibility of disruption to the journey, health problems or theft. As well as these precautions, what you do at the time in the face of any difficulties is also significant and affects the way you experience them and the consequences. Some 'accidents' could have been prevented by better preparation or more thoughtfulness. Moreover, tough going can have a positive side by providing learning opportunities that are better than just coasting along. This chapter considers what can go wrong, how you can prepare for it, how you can best handle it, and what you can do to help get back on track.

Links

Background information about your *Fellow travellers* ▷09–11.
Explanation of terms in *Language* ▷226–8.
The following topics have strong links with the themes in this chapter:
Learning agreement ▷24; *Placement diary* ▷33; *Ground rules* ▷50; *Codes of practice* ▷52; *Social networking* ▷74; *Recording supervision* ▷116; *Assessment* ▷123; *Wisdom of the group* ▷137; *Practice panels* ▷143; *Halo and horn effects* ▷200.
Examples of placement documents are indicated by ▷**W**, and can be downloaded at: www.routledge.com/textbooks/9780415499125

Preliminaries

First things first. Do you know at the start of the placement what you would do if, during the placement, things started to get difficult? Rather like knowing the local emergency number or the address of the consulate, it is always better to have this information to hand before it is needed. We consider the possible *protocols* for placement breakdown later in this chapter; for now just make sure that you know where to look and who to go to if things were to take a turn for the worse. What are the complaints procedures and what you can do if you are unhappy with the way the placement is going?

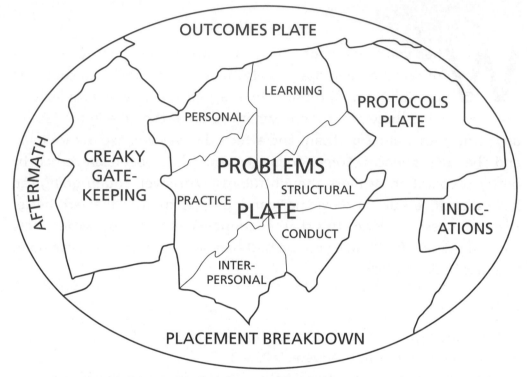

✦ *Chart 7.1: Tectonic plates of Socialworkworld*

Indications

Like the weather, there are usually signs that things might be about to deteriorate and it is important first to be able to read these signs, and second to know what to do about them.

☁ Early signs

From the student's perspective, you might notice that your supervisor is difficult to contact or, conversely, is not leaving you to find your own feet; perhaps it feels that the supervisor is dismissive of your concerns or seems to go at a very different pace from you.

From the supervisor's perspective, you might note that students make themselves scarce, tend to be late or unreliable. Perhaps they do not follow through an agreed plan or decision. You might feel that they have difficulty understanding their role or that they are slow to grasp opportunities in the placement.

Whatever the signs and whoever is experiencing them, it is important to check to see if it is just a one-off or whether there is a pattern developing. This is where the *Placement log* (▷33) is useful, because it gives you a time to check in with yourself and glance back over recent entries. If it does seem that it is more than a passing shower, you should talk with the person face-to-face and share your perception and concern with a view to finding out how they see it and to agree some changes. This opens communication channels and usually helps to prevent the situation from becoming critical. However, if no agreement is possible, or the agreed changes do not happen, then the bad weather has actually arrived and it is time to take further steps (see below).

Other signs

In Chapter 3 we considered a model to introduce *Direct observation* (▷63) and *Live teaching* (▷64), in which the responsibility for taking the lead in direct work with service users transfers gradually from supervisor to student, ideally with a period akin to co-working when supervisor and student are taking roughly equal responsibility for leading. This progress over time is represented by Student A in Chart 7.2 ▷150. How long this process takes and, indeed, whether any co-working happens at all, are also indicators of how well the placement is going.

The unbroken line shows a placement in which, for whatever reason, the process is much slower. Student B is beginning to take the lead much later in the placement than Student A and no co-working has been possible. There would be concerns with Student B, but the general direction is still favourable, so there could be continuing hope that the student might still achieve 'lift-off' even if it will take more time. With Student C the direction has taken a downward track, with the supervisor having once again to pick up the lead. Student C is unlikely to be able to retrieve the situation and is at risk of failing the placement.

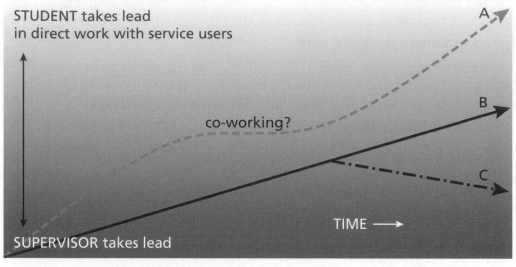

STUDENT takes lead
in direct work with service users

A

co-working?

B

C

TIME →

SUPERVISOR takes lead

✦ *Chart 7.2: Indicators of progress*

What can go wrong?

There are many different ways in which a placement can head off the rails. The typology below does not in itself provide solutions, but a careful analysis of the problem is the starting point to help decide on a solution, so use this typology to begin that analysis.

💣 Problems with practice

Not what the student wanted

Placement finding (▷38) frequently requires compromises. Some students are more adaptable and/or have fewer commitments than others, and some placements genuinely offer more scope than others. Very occasionally it turns out that some placements are a little too *Off the beaten track* (▷171–191) and it becomes clear that there is not the range of opportunities needed to meet the learning objectives; in most cases this would be picked up through the negotiation of the *Learning agreement* (▷24) and other safeguards put in place, or there might be a decision not to use the site as a placement.

Poor practice

The quality of the practice itself can be a cause for concern. Is it your practice as a student that is causing concern or the practice in the placement more generally, or perhaps a combination of the two? As we saw in *Writing up* (▷141), it is important for all concerned to document the placement clearly; if there are concerns, there need to be specific examples of what the causes for this are, a clear exposition of why they are causing problems and what people have tried to do so far to work with them. Often the very process of documenting the difficulties can help to pave the way to a solution. If not, it will be necessary to turn to the *Protocols* (▷163).

A QUESTION OF INTEGRITY

I'd been in the placement just over a week and I'd been troubled by some of the comments I'd heard. One was about gays, and was hard to challenge because it was told in the form of a 'joke' and I'd only just started and didn't want to seem pompous. But then someone mentioned that when my supervisor first started working there she'd been given a pile of assessments to do by the end of her first month, and when she'd said there was no way she could see all these people in the time available they said, 'oh, just do the assessments and then see them later – otherwise we won't meet our targets in time and we'll be financially penalised.' I couldn't see what a placement with so little integrity could teach me.

Nat Davies, student

Nat's experience begs many questions about the tension between professional integrity and organisational pressures and where we are prepared to draw the line. There are also some practical issues such as how Nat might verify the information to which he has become privy (he has not heard it direct from the supervisor) and how this kind of dilemma might be useful learning even if it is not good practice. Nat is not seeking employment there, merely to be able to learn about practice. How might he use the fact that he is a student rather than an employee; and at what stage might he think there is a need for *Whistle-blowing* (▷167)?

☀ Problems with learning

Mindset

💬 DOOR 1	MINDSET	DOOR 2 💬
I really struggled to see what this placement could offer me. After a couple of weeks I brought it up in supervision – that I'd really like to let my supervisor know what I'd done in my previous work in some detail – not to brag about it, but so I felt she could understand me better. She listened carefully, which made me feel like my experience was valued; it also helped me to listen to what my supervisor had to say – about how it can be difficult to see yourself as 'a student' when you've got lots of experience, but how she would like to see me throw myself into the role. She said *she* still felt she wore 'L' plates and that it was the sign of a good worker always to be curious and self-questioning. I liked that. *Brenda Shapiro, student*		I really struggled to see what this placement could offer me. I'm an experienced social care worker and I don't need to be shown the ropes like a baby social worker. It made me very angry but my supervisor's got the power of pass/fail so I just sat on it and thought 'oh, well, I'll put up with it and play by the rules.' After a while she brought up in supervision how she didn't think I was 'soaking it up'; she implied I wasn't open to learning. I zipped it at first but then all the resentment came boiling up and I lost it; I told her straight how the placement offered me nothing because I was already so experienced and no one acknowledged that. Next thing I knew it all came apart and the placement broke down. *Brenda Shapiro, student*

The significance of *mindset* (the attitude and approach that you have towards the placement) cannot be emphasised too much (▷*Preliminaries*, 54; *Mindset*, 120). This is not to suggest that you should put up with anything, but it does imply that the learning is there to be *discovered* as much as it is there to be offered on a plate. Brenda's story highlights the consequences of different mindsets, not just about the placement but also how you feel about yourself and your willingness to see yourself as an active participant who can change the course of events – sometimes called the locus of control (🕮1). 'The more I study, the better results I get' shows a belief in an *internal* locus of control; 'it doesn't matter how much I study, the lecturer doesn't like me so I know I'll get a poor mark' reflects an *external* locus of control. Door 1 Brenda is assertive and takes the initiative and the results show. Door 2 Brenda sees the locus of control as being outside herself, with catastrophic results. The supervisor is the same person in both scenarios but the consequences for each Brenda could not be more different.

Lost in translation

Some students can translate action into written form with relative ease and others find this process difficult. *Doing* is a very important part of social work, of course, but so is *writing* and *reflecting*. You and your supervisor might feel positive about your direct work with service users but find that this quality is lost in the transition to the written page. This might be in your reports for the agency or the portfolio and practice assignments for your assessment. It is important not to cover this up but to talk about the difficulty as soon as possible so that you can access whatever additional help is available. It is tempting to rationalise that the *doing* is the important part and the writing less so; however, this is not the case. Service users will be sold short if you are not able to translate their concerns, desires and situations for others (via court reports, for example) in a clear, concise and accurate fashion.

Learning difficulties

There are recognised learning difficulties which have an impact on your placement. Most common of these is *dyslexia*; if you have this diagnosed before you start the course that is a tremendous advantage, but some students only come to understand their difficulties as dyslexia after they are accepted to higher education. Some of the strategies that are used to compensate for dyslexia, such as having others do your writing, are useful only in the short term and more time and energy can be spent covering up than doing something about it. On placement you will have to write your own records, reports and portfolio, often without any intermediary, so it is your own abilities that are being tested; better that everyone knows what these are and, therefore, what additional help might be needed, well before the placement has started.

🗨 DOOR 1   HIDE AND SEEK   DOOR 2 🗨

I've never felt confident with my studies and I missed some schooling which, with my social work hat on, I now know was a form of school phobia. But I caught up with Access and I did well enough to apply for the social work course.

Tara Watson, student

I got a lot of help with my application form and when I did the written test I was showed up. I admitted I had difficulties, but they said I had potential. I was diagnosed dyslexic and I got a learning contract which gives me help with strategies and support from student services. Even with help it's a struggle and I knew it would be even harder on placement. There's not the same amount of support as at uni, but my supervisor is sympathetic – we discussed it right at the beginning and it was agreed I could have a bit more time to finish my reports and records.

Tara Watson, student

Over the years my cousin's helped me – it's still my work, it's just that she can make it look better. I've got the ability, but try getting other people to see it that way! I don't see why you need to write academic to do social work. I get coursework help off the internet, too. It worries me sick and it got so as on placement I just couldn't face it, kept being ill. It all came to a head when they said I'd copied a report, when all I'd done was use it to help me write mine. They said it was a question of integrity but they don't understand what it's like trying to hide it, your shame.

Tara Watson, student

●✲ Problems with conduct

Conduct, even more than competence, is a common reason for placements to break down. *Professional boundaries* (▷135) are a tricky area and it is important to take your lead from the supervisor about what is considered to be appropriate behaviour in the practice setting. Although there are some universal social work values (⊠1), the ways in which these are interpreted can vary from one work setting to another, depending on a variety of factors, not least the particular service user groups that you are working with. Research has also shown that different agencies and managers can interpret professional good conduct in different ways (⊠2). Some conduct issues come down to basic matters such as punctuality and reliability, but others are more complex. Discussing the student role early in supervision and completing the *Student boundaries* tour (▷46) means that you address these questions hypothetically in preparation for the possibility of the real thing. Whenever you have doubts or concerns about what is appropriate conduct, make sure you discuss these with your supervisor; and if your supervisor raises concerns about your conduct, listen carefully to the nature of these concerns. From your point of view there may be very good reasons why you are frequently not punctual, but your concern should be what you are going to do about it, not how you are going to excuse it.

💣 Personal problems

INTO MY OWN HANDS

I knew I was taking on a lot when I decided to retrain from teaching to social work – with family responsibilities, working part time and all the health problems that come from being a wheelchair user. It got to the point where I felt I was spinning plates on long poles and they were all about to drop on me. I decided that, rather than have all these plates drop on me as and when, I'd take things into my own hands – take the plates down myself, if you like. It was liberating. My supervisor and tutor didn't need or want to know the details of my personal troubles but accepted that I had been doing my best and that I needed time out. It was the best decision I made and though it made my studies longer than I wished, I felt it was better to aim for a success in the long term rather than a failure in the short term.

Shama Bindana, student

Demands of personal life

Students have lives outside placements, some supportive of their work on the course and others less so. Often the greatest pressures come from balancing the demands of paid employment, childcare and family responsibilities with those of the placement. If the balance goes seriously out of kilter, this can threaten the success of the placement. It is important to respect *Supervisory boundaries* (▷110), so it is possible to discuss the threat to the placement without necessarily disclosing the specific details of your personal life; only in this way can the various avenues be explored for a decision that has due regard for all concerned – you, your family, the social work programme, your supervisor, the practice site and the service users.

Health and mental health problems

Another specific area of your life outside the placement that might have an impact on the placement is your health. If ill health has meant absences from the placement, a plan will need to be made as to how the time that has been lost to the illness will be retrieved, using the *Placement protocols* ($\triangleright$163). Can these be accommodated within the current placement with an extension or does this have too severe an impact on the next part of the programme? Most courses are tightly structured because of the scale of the curriculum that needs to be accommodated, leaving little room for manoeuvre. If the days lost are significant, an *intermission* to the next year of the programme may be the only practical step.

Crisis of confidence

Has there been a particular episode during the placement that has led to a collapse in your confidence or is it a more pervasive feeling that clouds everything? The former would suggest a temporary crisis that is capable of resolution, depending on the nature of the particular episode; the latter is likely to take longer to solve, with a risk that it becomes chronic and not contained. As with all personal problems, it is important to share the impact that any difficulties are having on your studies with your supervisor, not necessarily to discuss the nature of the personal problems but how they are likely to affect you on placement and, therefore, to help you both decide what to do.

💣 Interpersonal problems

Clashes

There are many reasons why student and supervisor might not hit it off. Sometimes these might be exacerbated by different biographies (gender, race, etc) and might arise from differences in personal style or ideological outlook. Sometimes relatively small incidents, such as a mishandled or poorly received piece of feedback, or a jump to an unjustified conclusion, can lead the supervisory relationship into a vicious circle of distrust. Unless you talk about these differences as soon as there are indications, you each become sensitised to criticism, and the problems worsen.

Communication difficulties

In some ways all of the possible problems outlined so far have communication difficulties at their core, though these difficulties might have very different starting points. If the communication difficulties lie outside the supervisory relationship (with another member of the team, for example) they can more easily be openly discussed with the supervisor. It is more difficult when these problems lie between student and supervisor, but even more important that they are confronted.

💣 Structural and cultural problems

To what extent are the problems located at the personal and interpersonal level and to what extent are they more structural or cultural? More often than not, this is not an either/or but the problems spill back and forth between both of these areas, making it all the more complex to disentangle them.

Cultural sensitivity is a core social work value, but what this means in practice is complex. Take Scenario 3 in the *Professional conduct* tour (▷135), in which the particular religious beliefs of a student or social worker lead them to refuse to work with a same-sex couple. You may think that the response to this is obvious, but a research study found an enormous range of opinion as to what action, if any, should be taken in these circumstances (⌷2). Don't assume that your own response is the same as the response of your supervisor, your colleagues or the agency; any difference does not mean that you are right or wrong, but it does indicate that it could be problematic if it is not discussed.

Problems arising from racism, sexism or any other forms of discrimination that cannot be resolved person-to-person may make it necessary to resort to the agency's own complaints procedures and codes of conduct (▷*Protocols*, 163).

🚍 Defusing placement time bombs

A central message in the guide is the importance of being active at every stage of your placement and this is especially important around any time bombs. The significant word is 'time', not 'bomb'! There is a fuse and, as such, it can be *defused* before it becomes catastrophic.

The first significant step in this active approach is a recognition by all parties that there *is* a time bomb. Perhaps the most dangerous situation is when no one is aware of it, though the most common is when only one party thinks there is a problem. It is crucial to communicate the fact that there is a problem and to secure agreement that there is one, even if there is not agreement about the precise nature of the problem at this stage.

It helps to have some kind of framework to shape what is likely to be a difficult discussion, whoever initiates it. Different perceptions are likely to stem from conflicts about where the difficulty lies: to what extent is it a case of the placement neglecting to provide adequate opportunities, for whatever reasons, or the student failing to make use of them – again, for whatever reasons. Chart 7.3 on page 160 shows one way of charting these perceptions with all the relevant parties. For example, the most extreme views, that one party is giving the placement their all and the other providing nothing, would be charted at either A6 or F1. Seeing where each of you is on the chart will, at least, give an immediate and graphic insight into how near or far your perceptions are from one another and, therefore, the distance that each of your understandings will need to travel and, therefore, the size of the potential time bomb.

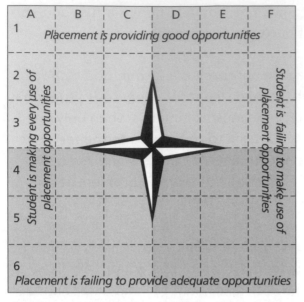

Placement is providing good opportunities

Student is making every use of placement opportunities

Student is failing to make use of placement opportunities

Placement is failing to provide adequate opportunities

✦ *Chart 7.3: Student-placement matrix*

What is evident throughout the preceding consideration of possible placement problems is that communication is vital. If needs be, talk about the difficulties with a friend or colleague first in order to achieve a better understanding of the nature of the communication difficulties. However, this is only helpful if you approach this in the spirit of enquiry about what might be happening, and therefore what you might do about it. If all you want is a cheerleader who will sympathise and confirm that you are doing the right thing, this might make you feel temporarily better but it will not help you defuse the bomb.

Creaky gate-keeping

Nobody wants you to fail your placement. Nevertheless, the placement is there not just to help you learn about practice but, as we saw in the previous chapter, as a testing ground, too. Ultimately, it is part of the gate-keeping process that ensures that service users can feel confident that their social worker has been rigorously educated, trained and tested. Thus, there are some circumstances in which the gate to the profession needs to be closed – firmly and fairly. In other words, it should not be taken for granted that the gate always allows passage, but there are many reasons why the gate might be creaky and difficult to close.

Emotional connection

Supervisor and student are generally thrown together in a relatively tight embrace on placement – like it or not – and the experience has an emotional dimension overlaying the educational and professional ones. It is a mistake to assume that these emotions are always negative when the gate is being closed; this is often the case, but there can be a strong positive connection which makes it all the more difficult for the supervisor to recommend this course of action. The struggle to avoid the closed gate can make the final decision all the more painful for everyone involved and might contravene the supervisor's social work philosophy based on an optimistic belief in the potential for change.

Feelings of personal failure as a supervisor

No matter how confident you are as a supervisor, It is natural to wonder whether there was something different that you could have done that would have helped the student through the gate. Feelings that the student's failure will reflect on the supervisor as failing, too, undoubtedly make it more difficult to make the fail recommendation. No placement is perfect (for example, perhaps it started late) and it can be difficult to disentangle factors relating to the placement with factors relating to the student. A supervisor who is not trained in social work might also lack confidence to make this kind of judgement.

Difficulty gathering evidence

Social work practice is not science; there is some considerable distance between excellent practice on the one hand and practice that is not good enough on the other; in other words, there are wide grey areas. Although we have been referring to a *closed* gate, we should more accurately speak of a *closing* gate; in other words, failure is a process whose direction can be reversed, the door can begin to open rather than continue to close, especially as there is always the hope that the student's learning and practice can improve to justify squeezing through. Getting evidence that justifies the shutting of the gate is a time-consuming and painstaking labour. Partly this is explained by the general presumption that the gate is open and that *negative* evidence has to be accumulated in order to justify a recommendation that it be closed. However, service users might properly expect that the gate is presumed shut and only opened when there is *positive* evidence to justify passage.

How high the bar?

We have been using the gate as a metaphor, but if we now think of the gate as a bar, we can begin to see the difficulty in judging how high or low the bar should be (▷*Chart 6.3 Height of the bar*, 130). No matter how many *performance indicators* are spelled out for each element, unit and key skill of the *Occupational Standards* (▷19), these still require skilled interpretation and it is natural to wonder whether you are being rather more demanding than other supervisors. Indeed, it is important to be open to the possibility that you *are* setting the bar too high.

Power politics

Justified or not, there can be a belief that the university will not be supportive of any attempts to close the gate. Failing the student will be seen as problematic, not least because student pass rates are important to the university's reputation. Even if relations with the individual tutor are close and trusting, the university establishment tends to be ambivalent towards professional bodies and the agencies that its vocational courses so heavily rely on. The placement is the space where these two worlds meet – or collide. Any question of the one (the practice site) making a judgement that is traditionally made by the other (the university) can be fraught. Practice sites will be reminded that it is the university's Examination board (▷*Practice panel*, 143) that makes the formal decision and that the supervisor's judgement is a *recommendation*. Attempts to close the gate can, therefore, test the partnership between agency and academy.

Knowledge of the consequences

There are many *Possible outcomes* (▷167) of these situations and the knowledge of the consequences for the student sometimes deters people from deciding that the gate should be closed. This is especially the case when the student has many personal and financial commitments that the supervisor is aware of, or when the supervisor knows what a personal struggle it has been for the student to achieve as much as they have, even if it is falling short of good enough.

Strengths and weaknesses

There are likely to be areas of strength as well as weakness and considerations about whether the areas of strength are such that they can compensate for the weaknesses. As we discovered in Chapter 6, competence is not an average (strengths + weaknesses ÷ 2). Nor should it be a blanket pass or fail. The nuances of a student's practice should be reflected in the report, so that standards that have been met do not have to be retested, but those that have not been met do.

Oiling the placement gate

The *Strengths and weaknesses* section above suggests that there is a need to *partialise* pass–fail judgements. This means that the judgement is not just a black-and-white pass–fail, but an acknowledgement of any aspects that have been satisfactory as well as those that will need to be reworked. This might, nonetheless, mean that the placement has been failed – and occasionally that the student is not suitable for social work and must leave the course – but in many cases it means an opportunity to consider what is needed to help students improve those areas of practice that have been identified as wanting. This more nuanced approach helps to 'oil' the gate that we have been describing because supervisors can say, 'well, I don't think the student is ready to pass through just yet, but these are the areas that are OK and these are the areas that need more work.'

Protocols for placement breakdown

Whatever the reasons for a placement breaking down, it is always a difficult experience for everyone; for those at the centre of the storm it can seem impossible that any learning could result, but it is helpful if you can hang on to this possibility.

We have already described how to recognise indications that things are not what they should be and made some suggestions about how they might be brought back on track. Informal action is normally the first step, with attempts to improve communication and make a plan for necessary changes. If this does not work, or any improvements are only temporary, the tutor should be involved in a meeting with student and supervisor(s) and possibly any other persons who have an interest, such as the supervisor's manager.

As the guide suggested early on (▷*Learning agreement* 24), you should know the protocols even if you do not need to invoke them.

🗁 Keeping a log

A *placement diary* (▷33) is an important part of your learning whatever the outcome, but it is indispensable if things are proving difficult. First, it might help to put the situation in perspective, as you give yourself time to reflect on your concerns and ways to handle them. Second, a documentary record of your experience of the placement can be presented as evidence if the enquiry becomes more formal. This is true of students, supervisors and anyone else involved in the placement; supervisors may not think to keep a log as such, but a regular reflection on your experience as a supervisor is helpful to your professional development, without it necessarily forming part of any later 'evidence'.

TAKING CONTROL

Although it wasn't the placement I'd have chosen, I thought I saw the potential in it; as it was a community-based project I also felt it would be a chance to do something a bit different. My supervisor went off sick quite soon after I arrived and the person who replaced him was a mixture of very bossy and controlling and then out of sight for days on end. I didn't have enough to do, but couldn't take the initiative either for fear of my controlling supervisor. It made me feel very insecure and perhaps someone with more experience than I've got would have found a way through it. I became very tearful, couldn't sleep and dreaded going in. It was really unfortunate but my off-site supervisor went off sick, too. I kept my placement diary up, at first as somewhere for all my feelings, but then more to keep a careful log of what happened – I logged my situation as 'B5' on the chart [Chart 7.3, ▷160]. I contacted my tutor, later than I should have, I know, but I felt such a failure and my supervisor was always so strong that I knew I'd find it hard to put my side of the case. From then things got better, not with the placement, but with me feeling more in control of events. The outcome was that I moved on to another placement; as my tutor said, 'You didn't fail the placement, the placement failed you.'

Mary O'Connor, student

Finding out what's wrong and why

Concerns meetings

The situation which Mary O'Connor describes in *Taking control* would trigger a 'concerns meeting'. In this case it is the student's concerns that have sparked the meeting, but any person involved in the placement can ask for one. A concerns meeting is more formal than a tutor visit and the findings from the meeting and any action plan arising from it will be carefully minuted and circulated.

Second opinions

Some programmes request an independent second opinion from an experienced supervisor, usually a trained practice teacher, to consider all the evidence available in order to make an adjudication. Second opinions are likely to be requested following a recommendation of fail or marginal practice.

Suitability meetings

In Chapter 6 the guide explored the different aspects of assessment, not just competence but also issues of *conduct* (▷134). Where there are concerns about a student's conduct the programme can call a meeting to discuss the student's suitability for social work. Each programme has its own protocols for suitability meetings, so make sure you are familiar with the course and placement handbook where you will find the details. (▷**w** for an example of the protocols for suitability meetings.)

Practice enquiries

An innovative way to handle all concerns, wherever they originate and whatever stage they have reached, is the practice enquiry team. The team is composed of three members – an experienced practice teacher, a manager from one of the agencies in the partnership (other than where the placement is situated) and a tutor (but not the one involved in the placement). Each of the persons involved in the concern (usually the student, supervisor and tutor) is asked to address the same three questions and, in turn and on their own, to discuss their responses with the team:

➢ What has worked well in the placement?
➢ What has not worked well in the placement?
➢ What do you think should happen now?

Each panel draws its membership from a wider pool of potential members so that the learning from these experiences is shared and spread across the social work partnership. The decision of the practice enquiry team carries authority because of the weight of experience that the pool of members develop and because it is a visible partnership between academy, profession and agencies. The panel's recommendation is made to the Examination Board.

An annual report by the person who convenes practice enquiry teams (the director of practice studies at the university, for example) can reveal any patterns in relation to placement concerns, and this assists the programme in identifying any structural problems (▷*Feedback, audit and monitoring*, 208).

☛ Whistle-blowing

Sometimes what is wrong concerns practice in the placement site itself. If you have concerns about any aspects of practice or management in the placement, it is crucial that you discuss these with your supervisor immediately to discuss what to do about them. Most agencies have whistle-blowing policies, which are designed to encourage staff to come forward rather than to cover for colleagues (⚇2). It is also possible to make a complaint to the regulatory body for social work, the General Social Care Council (GSCC) if policy, practice or procedure contravenes the GSCC codes of practice (there are codes for individual practitioners and for employers) (▱1). If your concern is actually about your supervisor's conduct and it is something you cannot discuss with the supervisor directly, your first contact should be with your tutor.

Possible outcomes

There are many possible outcomes to the meetings that will have taken place about the placement concerns. You may continue in your current placement for the rest of the time agreed, or for a lengthened period, most probably with a placement plan that addresses the concerns that have been identified. You may be offered a different placement, either as a continuation of the current period or in the near future; again, this might be to make up the days that are left, or a full new placement might be offered. It might have been agreed that a period of intermission is needed, so that you temporarily leave the course but with an expectation that you will return, perhaps when the circumstances that have halted the current studies have passed or been resolved.

There are some circumstances in which you might have to terminate your studies. If so, you need to ask yourself whether you think that everyone is suitable for social work? The answer, clearly, is no. Some people are not suited to it, so you have to think carefully whether you are one of these people. It need not be a reflection on the person you are, though it is bound to feel that way at first. However, if the person or people who have been charged with guiding and testing your learning and practice have come to a conclusion that it is not good enough, or not yet good enough, you need to be able to hear that message and reflect on it. No matter how fair or unfair you consider this judgement to be, there will always be reasons why the judgement has been made and you need to think how those reasons relate to your practice, your learning and your behaviour (☷3).

Aftermath

Much will depend on the way that the placement difficulties have been handled, how they came to light and, of course, the outcome – but it is very likely that feelings will be raw. Everybody who is involved in the process of questioning a placement or a student's practice will have spent much time and emotional energy in the process. In time, you will probably be able to reflect on the learning that these kinds of experience invariably allow, but it will usually take some distance from events before this is possible.

A recurring theme through the guide has been the different courses our lives can take (Path 1, Path 2, etc). Once the emotions of a failed placement are less raw, try to think about what 'Doors' might have been available to you and others in the placement – those critical points when a different decision or action might have turned events in a very different direction. Of course, this is hindsight, but in one sense our futures are guided by the wisdom of our collective hindsight.

For a practice site the aftermath of a difficult placement can be traumatic, especially for the supervisor (☷4). It is important to find ways to debrief and then to begin to put the experience into perspective, in particular to hold on to the knowledge that the vast majority of placements are positive experiences in which the student contributes much to the life and work of the practice site. The *Halo and horn effects* of past students are documented in a later chapter (▷200).

The consequences of placement failure for students who are also employees, in other words people who have been trying to make their workplace into a placement, are particularly devastating. This is another reason why these kinds of work-based learning experiences need to be carefully considered before they begin. Evidence used in the assessment of all students, but especially with regard to work-based study, needs to be 'triangulated' so that there are as many sources of evidence as possible ≋5.

✪ Boredom

A placement might not result in an actual time bomb such as those discussed in this chapter, yet it might not be fulfilling its potential. Less dramatic than the sudden crisis, but more insidious, is this 'slow crisis' that arises from boredom in a placement. The first question to ask yourself is whether there are any initiatives that you can take yourself as a student to pep up a slow placement; might the supervisor have underestimated your ability, energy or capacity? Talk it through with the supervisor and make your own suggestions for how you consider you could contribute more and, therefore, how the placement could give you more back in return.

If this draws a hostile or unenthusiastic response from your supervisor, do go back to your tutor to solicit their understanding and support, either to redraw your current placement or to seek an alterative. Usually it is question of (mis)judgement, but not always. Do not be tempted to ride the placement out, thinking that having too little to do seems like an attractive soft option; your time on placement is too valuable to spend it coasting along.

⊠ Click to download

⊠1 For guidance on codes of conduct ▷53⊠4
⊠2 GSCC Professional Boundaries study (2009) ▷ www.gscc.org.uk

▓ Books, articles, research reports

▓1   The notion of locus of control:
   ▷ Rotter, J.B. (1966), 'Generalized expectancies for internal versus external control of reinforcement', *Psychological Monographs*, 80. It has been further developed:
   ▷ Rotter, J.B. (1990), 'Internal versus external control of reinforcement: A case history of a variable', *American Psychologist*, 45, pp489–93.

▓2   These books have examples of whistle-blowing policies and activities:
   ▷ Ells, P., and Dehn, G. (2001), 'Whistleblowing: public concern at work', in C. Cull and J. Roche (eds) *The Law and Social Work*, Houndmills, Basingstoke: Palgrave.
   ▷ Hunt, G. (ed.) (1998), *Whistleblowing in the Social Services: Public Accountability and Professional Practice*, London: Edward Arnold.
   ▷ Hunt, G. (ed.) (1995), *Whistleblowing in the Health Service*, London: Edward Arnold.

▓3   Further insights into situations where the going gets tough:
   ▷ Sharp, M. and Danbury, H. (1999), *The Management of failing DipSW Students: Activities and Exercises to Prepare Practice Teachers for Work with Failing Students*, Aldershot: Ashgate.

▓4   ▷ Basnett, F. (2008), 'The impact of social work student failure upon practice teachers', unpublished report, Staffordshire University.

▓5   ▷ Williams, S. and Rutter, L. (2007), *Enabling and Assessing Work-Based Learning for Social Work: Supporting the Development of Professional Practice*, Learn to Care Publication 10. Birmingham: Learn to Care. www.learntocare.org.uk
   ▷ Shardlow, S.M. and Doel, M. (1996), *Practice Learning and Teaching*, Basingstoke: Macmillan.

CHAPTER EIGHT

OFF THE BEATEN TRACK

Social workers increasingly find themselves employed in settings where no one speaks 'social work'. Placements are being developed in schools and other educational institutions, in a wide variety of health care settings and in the criminal justice field, such as prisons and police. In addition, placements in community settings, with community groups and with service user and carer-led organisations, are a growing feature. These settings can offer excellent opportunities for students, but there are also challenges, not least the fact that the person who supervises the student day-to-day in the placement is unlikely to be a qualified social worker. As the supervisor guides the student around a parallel land, how are these experiences related to *Socialworkland* (▷xviii–xix)? This chapter explores the delights and the pitfalls of going off the beaten track into *non-traditional placements* and suggests how everybody can get the best from them.

Links

Background information about your *Fellow travellers* ▷09–11.
More explanation of terms in *Language* ▷226–8.
The following topics have strong links with the themes in this chapter:
Specialist destinations ▷07; *Student role* ▷47; *Co-placements* ▷51;
Practice curriculum ▷80; *On- and off-site supervisors* ▷142; *Boredom*
▷169; *New and experienced supervisors* ▷202; *Supporting and sustaining placements* ▷213; *Do you speak social work?* ▷215.
Examples of placement documents are indicated by ▷**W**, and can be downloaded at: www.routledge.com/textbooks/9780415499125

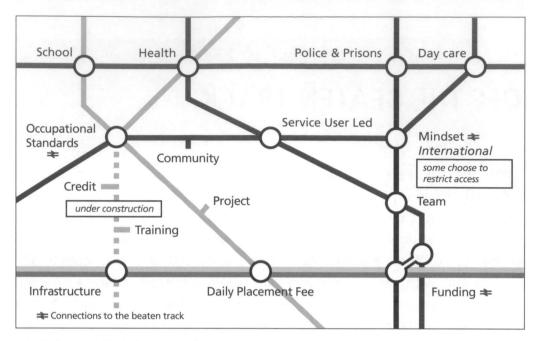

School   Health   Police & Prisons   Day care

Occupational
Standards
⇌

Service User Led

Community

Mindset ⇌
International

some choose to
restrict access

Credit ▬

under construction

Project

Team

▬ Training

Infrastructure

Daily Placement Fee

Funding ⇌

⇌ Connections to the beaten track

✦ *Chart 8.1 Practice-learning metro*

Preliminaries

TIME WAS ...

I qualified as a social worker in the 1970s. I had three placements
and two of them were what you'd now call 'non-traditional', though
we didn't think of it that way back then. One was in a probation
service, at a time when social workers and probation officers were
being educated together. I was the probation officer's first student,
and he was very enthusiastic. And then another placement was in
the residential unit of an adolescent psychiatric hospital, where my
supervisor was the psychiatrist. They were very good placements – I
can remember them as if it were yesterday – and gave me a really
rounded view of social work. If anything, they were better organised
than my third 'traditional' placement in the social services
department.

Viv Delaney, practice development manager

Off-the-beaten-track placements are often referred to as *non-traditional*, but in some ways they recapture a lost tradition of placements in alternative settings, as Viv describes in *Time was ...* . A placement might be considered non-traditional because it is not in a social work setting (e.g. it is in education, health or criminal justice), because it is not in the *statutory sector* (▷227) – though it should be remembered that some statutory functions are carried out in the voluntary sector – or because it is not in an established agency or organisation, as in the case of street work or placements with service user groups and neighbourhood groups. Although there are tremendous opportunities for learning in these kinds of placement, it is important to ensure that students and practice sites are well prepared, especially in terms of an understanding of how and where the 'social work' will be found.

But is it social work?

The first step when going off the beaten track is to allow yourself to believe that social work can be happening even in the absence of employed social workers or when 'it' is not called social work. So the question is not solely *do the opportunities for learning exist in this potential placement?* but *can I see them?* and, indeed, *how might I create them?* This mindset – the way in which you see the placement – is critical, as we have noted in so many other places in the guide.

How you define social work has a big impression on how you will see it (or not) in your placement (≋1). Definitions of social work such as the one that has been agreed internationally by the International Federation of Social Work (IFSW) (⊠1) are helpful in this respect, as are the accounts of people who use social work services (≋2). As we will see later, many off-the-beaten track placements use the *National Occupational Standards* (▷19) as a kind of dictionary to help translate the placement experiences into the language of social work learning. It is also the case that even students in 'traditional' placements can be puzzled by the fact that 'no one speaks social work' as they understand it from their college studies (▷*Do you speak social work?* 215).

Undoubtedly, some students find it easier to open themselves to these experiences, and some students are more adept at making the necessary translation of experience into social work learning. The same is true of the supervisors in these placements. However, none of these is a 'given' and the good news is that it is possible to transform mindsets and to develop skills. The rest of this chapter considers how to do this.

TARA COMPARES MINDSETS

Three of us were placed at *Links* – a service user neighbourhood group – and the placement was about working with the group to make a video about who the group were and what they did. Me and Leila thought this placement was the best thing, I mean we really learned so much and enjoyed it – great! But Jenny, she was the other student, and she couldn't make anything of it, couldn't really get into it at all and thought it was a waste of time. Fact is, it was her that wasted the time.

Tara Watson, student

Examples of placements off the beaten track

What do we mean by *non-traditional*? Let us consider some specific examples; the following come from a research project which explored what creates successful non-traditional placements and how this success can be sustained (⊠2; ▷*Backpacking: placements abroad*, 188):

➤ *prisons and police* (⊠3)
➤ *an independent fostering agency* for children with emotional and behavioural difficulties
➤ *a rural hosting scheme* where students from an urban-based university undertake placements in the statutory, voluntary and independent sectors in one of two neighbouring rural counties
➤ *school* placements with special educational needs coordinators
➤ *school mentors* – placements with school mentors and in early years projects
➤ *estranged children and families* – a private company working with children and families who are estranged from one another

> *community living (mental health)* – a small voluntary organisation working with African/Caribbean people aged 17 years with mental health difficulties
> *independent living (learning disabilities)* – placements with service users with learning disabilities with the aim of building community participation
> *interprofessional learning in children's centres* – placements for social work and nursing students together in ten children's centres across a city and neighbouring county
> *HIV/AIDS project* – a small service-user led charity offering social and psychological support to those infected by, and affected by, HIV/AIDS
> *service users support (mental health)* – a service-user-led project for people with mental health problems
> *asylum seekers mental health project*   a community action project with asylum seekers, refugees and also with people with mental health problems
> *service users and carers in domiciliary and daycare settings*
> *a consortium of voluntary sector agencies (80 in all)* – able to place students in a wide variety of voluntary sector organisations.

Although none of these sites had social work in the title, and very few employed social workers, they had all developed successful opportunities for social work students. Importantly, they were sustaining themselves as placements well beyond the first flush of the pilot stage. What follows explores the factors that help these placements to become successful.

⚲ Added value of students

You are a positive asset to a non-traditional placement. In a survey of these placements (⌂2), student social workers were noted as adding value to the practice site in several possible ways, as described below:

> You have personal qualities such as innovation and energy that benefit the practice site.
> You have a bit more time to spend with people who use the services.
> You might develop a new service, or expand an existing one, such as starting up and leading a new group; or gather new information, often through project work.

> You can bring a social work perspective to the practice site, helping regular staff to rethink their practice and place it in a wider context.
> You can bring up-to-date knowledge, for example in terms of new legislation or practice methods.
> The fact that placements are offered and supervised can benefit the site's image, perhaps being used in publicity and improving recruitment potential.

The points above are all positive assets which, ironically, might be less easy to find or achieve in a traditional placement setting. However, you do need to be aware of these possible expectations before you start the placement so they can be discussed to see what they might mean in practice. Shama's experience shows the importance of a continuing dialogue with your supervisor (▷*Valuable resource or unpaid labour?*, below).

VALUABLE RESOURCE OR UNPAID LABOUR?

I spent a day at *FamilyLinks*, them getting to know me and me them before we all decided 'yes, let's go ahead with the placement.' I was the first social work student they'd ever had, and it did make me feel a bit special – bit of a guinea pig, too. My supervisor had done a three-day course and he had a mentor, which was good, and I saw my off-site practice educator once a fortnight. My supervisor asked if I would do a session with the volunteers on the Disability Discrimination Act from the point of view of a wheelchair user and I was happy to do this. He thought it would appeal to the teacher in me – he knew that I'd trained as one – and he was right. Then he asked me to facilitate a series of sessions with the paid staff about social work. These were well received and everyone was appreciative, but it took a lot of time to prepare them and I was getting behind with my coursework. It was when I was asked to organise an ethnic awareness day that I decided that 'feeling useful' had turned into 'being used'. I went online to my network group (my practice educator was on holiday) and they supported me to talk to my supervisor about how I felt. It turned out OK – I think he'd been acting out of the best motives and he was genuinely sorry that it'd got too much.

Shama Bindana, student

♀ Preparation

These sites are off the beaten track in social work terms and they are relatively new to social work learning, so it is essential that there is thorough preparation for the site as well as for the individual student. Not surprisingly, teaching and learning materials figure strongly as important to preparing sites in this way; 69 per cent of respondents in a study of non-traditional sites (⬚2) made specific reference to induction packs and training materials as part of their preparation. Training and careful briefings for work-based supervisors were highlighted and, of course, making sure you have a desk, a computer and library resources.

Work-based supervisors who are new to this role will need support, usually from a mentor, but also from the rest of the team or unit with whom they work.

A TEAM AFFAIR

We prepare agencies to think through how they will support the development of a professional social work identity in a non-social work setting, and an important part of this is for the practice site to see a placement as a *whole team* experience so it is not just the work-based supervisor who is carrying the responsibility for the student's learning opportunities. All the parties need to have confidence in the site's ability to provide appropriate learning opportunities.

Advance publicity at university open days is recommended and, of course, preparatory meetings for potential students with team members and service users – longer, all-day pre-placement visits are much better at giving everyone a better idea of the placement's potential and the likely fit with the student. I think most important of all, we provide a mentor for small groups of work-based supervisors *in advance* of the actual placement of a student.

Sandra Townsend, director of practice studies

How students learn off the beaten track

How might you expect to learn about social work in a setting which is 'not social work'? In answering this question, you need to remember that, though these sites are off the main track in terms of social work, they usually have considerable experience of what they do, with no shortage of activities for you to get involved in. So, what kinds of activity are likely in these kinds of setting? The responses to the research study (⊠2) covered a wide range of activities and these are listed below, with the most frequent first:

➢ direct work with people who use the service
➢ assessment, planning, intervention, reviews
➢ teamwork, meeting work
➢ written work such as recording, reports, policy documents, minuting
➢ work with other professions, networks and agencies
➢ project work, new initiatives, event organising, research work
➢ groupwork
➢ taking on a supervisory role with service users
➢ taking part in agency-based training workshops
➢ observation, shadowing, buddying.

It is interesting and perhaps reassuring to note that this is pretty much the kind of list that you would expect from a traditional placement. There are perhaps more activities involving project work. An example is a project to increase the involvement of black and minority ethnic communities in service user participation. This was undertaken by a student in a mental health support placement. However, the kind of kit described in Chapter 3 seems relevant to all sites for social work practice learning, whether on or off the beaten path. Indeed, opportunities for *live teaching* (▷64) and *direct observation* of your practice and learning (▷63) might be more common in the community, day and residential settings that characterise these off-the-beaten-track placements.

THE AMBASSADOR

Some of the other students on the course were going, 'what good's a placement in a school, there's no jobs in it for social workers?', but I said I wanted somewhere where I'd be face-to-face 80 per cent and face-to-computer 20 per cent, not the other way round. And I was right. It's a brilliant placement – knew it would be as soon as I had the preparation day. I work with different ages of students (pupils), sometimes with their parents, too. I've learned a whole new problem-solving method that really works – I'll take that with me, and the confidence that's come with it, wherever I go to work in the future. I think I've learned more about social work in a so-called 'non-social work' setting than a lot of the others have learned in their 'social work' ones, which is perhaps a bit sad. I see a lot more of my supervisor (and she sees a lot more of me in direct work) than lots of the students who've been in more mainstream placements. And I know that it *is* possible to find a job where I'm working with people most of the time and not with assessment forms. Personally, I think all students should complete their training with this kind of expectation of professional standards. My supervisor said, 'you're like an ambassador for *real* social work!' and though she was kind of joking, she's right. That's how I feel after this placement.

Mary O'Connor, student

Translating activities into learning

How do practice sites with no qualified social work staff begin to understand what social work is, never mind help students to develop their learning of it? And how are the activities we listed earlier actually transformed into social work learning? A study points to the significance of the *National Occupational Standards* (▷19) for social work to unlock this understanding (▱2).

⚲ Using the national occupational standards (NOS)

THE INTERPRETER

💬

I mentioned before what a boon the National Occupational Standards were (NOSs). They helped me see how the experiences I can offer as a service user who manages her own budget relate to the learning needs of a student on placement with me (▷22). I'm so familiar with the NOSs now that I'd almost forgotten what it's like when you first look at them; I remind myself this is how students feel at the beginning of their first placement. I don't want to take for granted all the work that my interpreter did (I called her that, because it always felt like she was translating one language into another!). She was actually my mentor and, along with the three days' training that I had with other supervisors who were new to social work placements, I don't know what I would have done without her to explain things in those early days. There are some NOSs that students probably can't meet on a placement with me, but that's OK – because we know what they are, we find other ways the students can meet these or that those NOSs are covered in a different placement.

Susan Chapman, service user

The challenge of converting the experience at the practice site into social work practice learning is considerably assisted by the explicit statements in the Occupational Standards for social work (▷19). Other professions such as teachers and health professionals are familiar with the notion of occupational standards, so this general understanding can be transferred to the specifics of the standards for social work. Even when the supervisor is not at all familiar with the idea of occupational standards, they provide a description of values, knowledge and skills that are both general and specific enough for lay people to understand readily – especially with the help of an *interpreter* to translate where necessary. It is particularly useful when the social work programme provides illustrative material which brings the individual standards to life. It is not only the practice site that finds this helpful – students do, too.

TOUR: VOCABULARY

TRANSLATING BETWEEN OCCUPATIONAL STANDARDS AND ACTIVITIES

UNIT 7 Support the development of networks to meet assessed needs and planned outcomes *(an interpretation for students who are placed with service users who are supervisors and who manage their own budgets).*

In this Unit you will be expected to demonstrate your ability to:	**Activities for the student to undertake**
➢ Examine (with individuals, families, carers, groups, communities and others) support networks which can be accessed and developed; ➢ Work with individuals, families, carers, groups, communities and others to initiate and sustain support networks; ➢ Contribute to the development and evaluation of support networks.	Complete a life history of and with the service user supervisor. *Listening, collaboration, presentation.* Meet with some of the workers involved with the service user and summarise potential useful collaboration and potential areas of conflict (e.g. in their organisation's policies). *Selection of specific information, communication.* Write a personal statement about which outcomes are achieved and how you could contribute to them. *Reflection, interpretation, identification.*

Students' work for the portfolio *[1000 Words]*

Reflecting on your practice learning experience, discuss how community and family networks are used to support service users within the placement setting.

➢ Identify the different organisations (statutory/voluntary/community) and family and individual networks that support the person you are placed with.

➢ Reflect on the outcomes to be achieved and who might contribute what to the process.

➢ Reflect on the way that people and professionals work together and where there are areas of conflict or potential conflict.

➢ Are the intended outcomes achieved or not? Reflect on your role in working with the person and how you might support them to achieve their goals.

With thanks to Elaine Flynn

The practice sites in the research study (⊠2) noted that the process of translation is not easy at first and benefits from the guidance of someone who is experienced in the language of social work and practice learning. As we see in the above tour, it is also helpful to know how the work you are expected to complete for your portfolio links with the occupational standards and with the experiences on placement.

Sustaining placements off the beaten track

It is one thing for a new and innovative development to get going, buoyed by the enthusiasm of a pilot, but another for it to be sustained beyond this initial impetus. Below we summarise what sustains these non-traditional placements as reported in the findings of a research study (⊠2).

⚲ Infrastructure

Socialworkland (▷xviii–xix; 79) maps the 'twin cities' of Practice and Learning, but what if these cities also had a vast subway system, a *Practice–Learning metro*? (▷Chart 8.1, 172). Although not evident to those on the surface, this unseen network is nevertheless vital to the functioning of Practice and Learning by enabling people and ideas to move around efficiently.

The success of placements depends more on this network than most individual students or supervisors are likely to appreciate. Of course, the commitment, hard work and abilities of students, supervisors and tutors is critical, but if placements are to be sustained – and non-traditional ones in particular – it is the robustness of these systems that can make the difference.

An increasingly systematic approach to supporting non-traditional placements seems to be emerging out of the more haphazard approaches that were identified in the early days of the social work degree in England (⊠4). It is as if the lines under construction on the Practice–Learning underground have been joined up. The dominant model seems to be for on-site supervisors to provide day-to-day oversight of the student's practice learning, supported by off-site practice educators who are experienced not just in social work but also in practice teaching. What is less systematic and needs greater attention is the training provided for work-based supervisors – it is patchy in terms of its duration, credit-rating and assessment. Some is not credit-rated or assessed at all. This makes it difficult to establish a direct line from placement-supervisor role to practice-educator role, for those who might like to see their professional development travel in that direction. Equally confusing is the wide range of terms used for these different roles (▷226), a confusion that prevents comparisons and is likely to inhibit the systematic development of social work practice learning.

This 'underground' network is increasingly staffed by people with time dedicated to finding, developing and supporting new sites for practice learning, and it has been critical to increasing both the quality and the quantity of placements overall. The work, for example in translating activities at the practice site into national occupational standards (and vice versa, translating standards into activities), has enabled many sites to develop the confidence and the expertise to offer placements.

⚷ Funding

Funding is a significant factor in sustaining placements, traditional and non-traditional. New funds from the UK government were used to appoint the staff who developed the infrastructure described in the previous section, and practice learning continues to be supported through the Daily Placement Fee (an amount given to the practice site for each day the student is on placement ▷05 *Currency*), which is another important element in sustaining the quantity and quality of practice learning opportunities. The political attention that the quality of placements attracted, largely as a result of well-publicised shortcomings in child protection, has undoubtedly helped to give placements a higher profile. This led to the funding of the Practice Learning Taskforce between 2003 and 2006 (⌧5) and to the inclusion of practice learning as one of the performance indicators by which local authorities were judged on their eligibility for central government funding (between 2004 and 2008). The fear is that once the political attention span is exhausted, the funding that has helped to develop and sustain social work practice learning will dry up.

♀ Groups

Groups play a significant part in providing peer support and learning for students, and groups for practice supervisors have potential, though they are not yet as developed as they might be. The relatively small size of some off-the-beaten-track placements (especially in local community groups) makes it particularly pertinent to develop group support, both for students and for groups of supervisors relatively new to this role. So, potential sites for practice learning need to consider what social work practice learning networks are available both for themselves and for their students. There are also implications for the demands that groups make on the facilitator's groupwork skills, as the facilitator may or may not be experienced in groupwork (▷*Group supervision* 112; ▣3).

♀ Credibility over time

Of course, going off the beaten track has plenty of challenges, as the study to which we have been referring discovered (▣2). In most cases it is a crisis of confidence that often arises from scepticism that the site can provide appropriate learning opportunities. We have already noted the role that the National Occupational Standards can play in providing a common language to bridge these concerns, as well as the significance of thorough preparation, training and support.

Those sites that persist beyond initial setbacks can usually achieve changes in the mindsets of all those involved. The belief in the added value of students is something that comes with time and experience. Confidence in the placement's capacity to deliver quality practice learning has to be earned over time. In terms of timing, non-traditional placements have to be particularly mindful of *when* they can make the best contribution to the student's learning – relatively earlier or relatively later in the student's time on the course? Three out of four sites in one research study (▣2) offered placements across the whole time span of studies, perhaps contrary to expectations that these non-traditional placements would tend to provide only a first or early placement.

TOUR: HOW TO SUSTAIN SOCIAL WORK LEARNING OFF THE BEATEN PATH

Eight guides to help sustain non-traditional sites for social work learning:

1 **Knowing where the 'social work' is**
   Students need to be helped to make connections with their learning whilst in this placement and the practice of social work. They need regular contact with off-site practice educators who are qualified social workers and are trained in practice teaching.

2 **Being open about expectations**
   Practice sites need to be open about their hopes for the student's presence; full-day preparatory contacts in which students have the opportunity to shadow workers and service users can help bring these expectations to the fore.

3 **'Translating' the National Occupational Standards (NOS)**
   Supervisors should know how to translate the NOS to their particular setting and which specific ones will be tested.

4 **Communication between supervisor, educator and tutor**
   Students need to feel confident that all involved in their practice education network are aware of each other's respective roles and responsibilities and that these are coordinated. Who is responsible for coordination?

5 **Combining individual and group support and supervision**
   Peer group support can assist students' learning. It should sit side by side with individual supervision, so that the one does not supplant the other.

6 **Timing the placement**
   Non-traditional sites in particular need to consider what they have to offer students at different points in their learning, and whether there is likely to be a preference between early and late in the student's career.

7 **Networking with other sites**
   Linking with sites that have successfully made the transition from novice to established provider of placements boosts know-how and confidence.

8 **Monitoring and evaluating the placement experience**
   The experiences of all involved should be gathered, analysed and acted upon.

Other important aspects, not necessarily within the control of the practice site, are the availability of training for supervisors and continued financial support for placements in non-traditional settings.

As noted in the *Infrastructure* section, the role of individual development workers and practice learning coordinators is critical in launching these sites to success and keeping them successful, and therefore to their growing credibility.

Placements on more than one site

It is quite possible that one particular practice site will not be able to meet all your learning needs. In discussion with your tutor you should be clear about whether your social work course expects you to complete all the occupational standards in each and every placement or whether you are able to satisfy some standards in one placement and others in another.

One way in which a good placement can still be used, even if it cannot deliver all of your learning needs, is to consider how you might have a placement on more than one site, so that between them they will meet your learning objectives. This can be an imaginative and fulfilling experience or a complicated and unmanageable disaster. To increase the chances of a successful placement, you should ensure that there is a preliminary meeting with your tutor and the supervisors from both sites, as well as any off-site coordinating supervisor. The meeting needs to answer the following questions.

- What learning objectives and occupational standards will be met in each site?
- What are the practical arrangements; for example, which days will be spent at which site and what are the hours at each site?
- How will the supervision arrangements be managed and who will be the overall coordinator for the supervision (perhaps an off-site supervisor)?
- What are your assessment arrangements in each site and how will they be coordinated?
- What would happen if one site was happy with your practice and the other not?

The main concern is that the two (or more) sites know what each other is doing, so there is regular communication between them that does not rely solely on you as the student.

Interprofessional placements

Many of the placements that are described as off the beaten track are in fact very much on a beaten track – it is just that the track is beaten by professions other than social work. These placements have the potential for interprofessional learning, though there is a difference between a social work placement that happens to be in a prison, a hospital or a school and one that is structured so that students of social work and probation, social work and health or social work and education actually learn together.

There is a debate to be had as to whether it is better for students first to develop their identities as social workers and, from that position of knowledge and strength, to reach out to other professional groups; or whether to have interprofessional learning from the very start, before lines get fixed and barriers erected. In the absence of research evidence, this question is answered more by belief and opinion than knowledge. Where do you stand? The answer is probably uncomfortably complex and may well differ from student to student, so that some would benefit from one approach and others from the other.

It is important to remember that interprofessional working is not some general mishmash of practice, a generic soup in which the professions are indistinguishable. Certainly, there are some skills and tasks that overlap between professional groups, as the new type of worker developments emphasise (◪6), but there are also important differences. Social workers have a uniquely holistic perspective on the people with whom they work, being educated to see the broader issues and to see individuals in their social and political context. This mission is undeniably under threat from the extreme forms of specialism to which the profession is currently subject. Asking yourself why you decided to train as a social worker and not, for instance, as a health visitor or a teacher, will help put you in touch with what you see as particular to social work. These differences are valuable and are the essence of what social work brings to the interprofessional table.

'Backpacking' – placements abroad

Some social work programmes give students the opportunity for study abroad. In some respects overseas placements are the 'backpackers' of practice learning, geographically and culturally very far from the beaten track. As such they have both much to offer and much to risk.

The first and main question to consider is *why* do you wish to undertake an international placement and what do you think it might offer you that is different from a domestic, local one. You need to consider the practical and financial implications of spending a period abroad, including medical and other insurance cover, accommodation and, of course, the language. Do you speak the language of the country to which you wish to go, do you have any opportunities to learn the language or can you be confident that English will be sufficient (as is often the case in some countries such as the Netherlands and in Scandinavia)? You are certainly likely to learn much about communication skills, and especially non-verbal communication.

THE WOULD-BE BACKPACKER

I had been attracted to this course because it offered quite a number of opportunities for an international placement. I spent six months in Chad before I came on the course and saw myself pretty much as a shoo-in for it. I was still keen, but as it got nearer the time and I put my request in, there were a few doubts. I was into a new relationship; it started just before I began the course, and I wasn't sure now that I wanted to be away from my partner for any stretch. But I realised that being a volunteer (as I was in Chad) was very different from being an assessed student. Actually, what crystallised it for me was an exercise that the international tutor did with us. There were various scenarios we discussed, which included this one: *You see adult workers, who are standing outside the placement smoking, talking to young people using the service who are also smoking; and you even see them handing out cigarettes to smoke there. The children are between 12 and 15. You have been taught that this is unacceptable here in the UK so what do you do about this, if anything? *
I realised that I wasn't temperamentally suited just now to hold back in the way I think you'd need to (call it arrogance) and so I decided not to push my application.

Nat Davies, student

* *With thanks to Janet Williams*

What preparation will you receive and do you expect from your home university? What arrangements for support and supervision will there be in the host university and practice site? This is easier when the placement is part of a formal partnership between your university and another (for instance, within the European Union, as part of an Erasmus programme). If it is a one-off arrangement, these need to be especially well researched. There may be particular requirements that you had not thought of (for instance, placements in any hospital in Sweden require students to be tested for MRSA). Bear in mind that, as an unusual person – as you likely will be on an international placement – you are an ambassador for social work and for your home university, so your behaviour and attitudes will be noted.

Especially important is to find out how the learning in the placement abroad fits with the rest of your course. For example, which occupational standards, if any, will need to be satisfied and how will the assessment be undertaken? You will need to be an autonomous and adaptable person to get the best from what international placements offer (it is not a holiday!) and be able to tolerate quite different mindsets and practices about what constitutes good social work practice (⫯4).

All of this guidance applies equally if you are an international student who is seeking or beginning a placement in the United Kingdom. The guide as a whole should give you an insight into the context of placements in the UK.

For useful websites ▷⊠7. Information about credit accumulation and transfer ▷204.

⊠ Click to download

⊠1 The International Federation of Social Workers (IFSW) definition of social work: ▷ www.ifsw.org/en/f38000138.html

⊠2 The research report, 'How new projects and initiatives in social work practice learning successfully mature': ▷ www.skillsforcare.org.uk

⊠3 A full review of placements with police and prisons:
    ▷ Miller, A. (2007), 'Developing Practice learning in police and prison services in the West Midlands': ▷ www.skillsforcare.org.uk

⊠4 Doel, M., Deacon, L. and Sawdon, C. (2004), *An audit of practice learning in the first year of the social work degree*, Practice Learning Taskforce: ▷ www.practicelearning.org.uk

⊠5 The Practice Learning Taskforce's publications, including the *Capturing the Learning* series are still available:
    ▷ www.practicelearning.org.uk

▱6 New Types of Worker (NTOW): ▷ www.newtypesofworker.co.uk
    For new types of placement:
    ▷ Doel, M. (2008), *Revisiting New Approaches to Practice Learning*,
      Leeds: Skills for Care and CWDC www.skillsforcare.org.uk
▱7 Websites for international travel:
    ▷ www.hstelbookers.com and www.inyourpocket.com
    Study in Europe website: ▷ www.study-in-europe.org
    The National Union of Students (NUS) Extra card:
    ▷ http://www.nusextra.co.uk/buy/

📚 Books, articles, research reports

📚1 These introductions to social work cover the range of social work.
    ▷ Payne, M. (2006), *What is Professional Social Work?* (2nd edition),
      Bristol: Policy Press.
    ▷ Shardlow, S.M. and Nelson, P. (eds) (2005), *Introducing Social
      Work*, Lyme Regis: Russell House.
📚2 The range of social work activity as seen through the eyes of those
    who have experienced it directly; especially useful for people who
    have not experienced social work, either as a service user or as a
    professional:
    ▷ Cree, V.E. and Davis, A. (2007), *Social Work: voices from the inside*,
      London: Routledge.
    ▷ Doel, M. and Best, L. (2008), *Experiencing Social Work: learning
      from service users*, London: Sage.
📚3 A useful guide to group supervision:
    ▷ Atherton, S. (2006), *Putting Group Learning into Practice*, West
      Midlands Learning Resource Network/Skills for Care.
📚4 The international context of placements and practice education:
    ▷ Shardlow S.M. and Doel M. (2002), *Learning to Practise Social
      Work: International Approaches*, London: Jessica Kingsley.

CHAPTER NINE

NEW & EXPERIENCED

How experienced a traveller are you? Or, if you are the host, is this the latest visitor in a long line of many or your very first? The degree of experience – of practice, of being a student, of placements offered or undertaken – has a big impact on those concerned, yet it is often overlooked as a factor. It is important to be explicit about the different standards that are expected from one placement to the next and the information that is passed between placements. This chapter will look at how a *placement bridge* can be built from one placement to another. It also considers the impact of the different kinds and amounts of students' practice and life experience on the placement.

Links

Background information about your *Fellow travellers* ▷09–11.
More explanation of terms in *Language* ▷226–8.
The following topics have strong links with the themes in this chapter:
Visa for practice learning ▷43; *Orientation* ▷48; *Work-based placements* ▷51; *Unicorns* 89; ▷*Wisdom of the group* 137; *Added value of students* ▷175; *Do you speak social work?* ▷215.
Examples of placement documents are indicated by ▷**W**, and can be downloaded at: www.routledge.com/textbooks/9780415499125

Preliminaries

There are two kinds of 'new and experienced' to consider. The first is *how new or experienced are you to social work?* The second is *how new or experienced are you as a student?* Taking the map of *Socialworkland* (▷xviii–xix) as a starting point, you could have experience of this landscape as an unqualified practitioner yet be a novice *visitor*. On the other hand, you could be new to this landscape but familiar with *visiting* – that is, experienced at study and the student role.

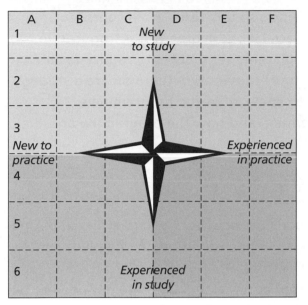

✦ Chart 9.1: New and experienced – locating yourself

Where would you put yourself on Chart 9.1? For example, if you were relatively experienced as a practitioner but very new to the student role you might put yourself around E1. There is no 'best' place to be on the map because there are advantages and disadvantages to each of the four quadrants. Consider the potential advantages and disadvantages of each quarter in turn. How can you make the best out of the position in which you have placed yourself and what might you have to look out for?

From placement to placement

One of the biggest challenges is to ensure that all the parts of the social work programme are 'joined up'. The obvious potential chasm is the one between class-based learning and practice-based learning – the *academy* and the *placement*. The guide considered how these can be best integrated in Chapter 4 (▷*Two vocabularies*, 85). However, one of the joins that does not always receive the attention it deserves is that between one placement and the next.

How many placements are there and when during the programme do they occur? Although the number of days on placement is prescribed (for example, in England it is a minimum of 200 in total), the ways in which the days are distributed is not, so this varies from course to course. The tendency since the social work degree was introduced in England in 2003–4 has been for placement numbers to reduce from three (and in at least one case, four) to two. Whether you are a student or a supervisor, it is important to know what the programme's expectations are for each placement, and how the programme and the placement relate to each other.

These are some of the significant questions to clarify:

➢ Are you expected to visit all parts of *Socialworkland* (▷xviii–xix) during each and every placement, or can some be visited on one placement and others during another?
➢ If some parts have been assessed as successful, do these not need to be revisited during a subsequent placement, and which aspects are these specifically?
➢ If some places have been visited but not to the satisfaction of the supervisor or others, how are these to be revisited differently the next time?

Information

Information from one placement should be available to the next one. Usually it is sufficient that the new supervisor has the information, but there should be discussion as to how widely in the placement team this information is shared. If the supervisor's colleagues in the team are to be involved in guiding you, then they need to know what strengths and weaknesses you bring as a student. In particular, if there have been any difficulties in the previous placement that now require a revisit, supervisors and their colleagues cannot be expected to guide and test you appropriately without detailed knowledge of why the revisit is needed.

Continuity in your learning and practice experience is aided by clear and concise documentation. This is another reason why a well-constructed *practice portfolio* (▷28) is essential to acquaint others, in plain English, with the story of your journey through the previous placement, and with clear distinctions between your descriptions, your analyses and your reflections. A person who does not yet know you well, such as your new supervisor, should be able to read the story of your previous placement and the judgements that have been made in such a way that they have a good sense of who you are now as a developing professional. They need to know about your progress through *Socialworkland*, where your strengths lie and where there is need for development, or even for some remedial work to catch up. So, though your placement documentation is confidential, it is not private; there are named people who will need to read it.

Standards

As we explained in Chapter 6, the setting of standards is not science and involves considerable judgement. However, in order to be as fair and consistent as possible, standards need to be based on criteria which are known beforehand and further developed together with the supervisor (▷*You need three legs for a stool*, 132). The level at which you are expected to practise should vary both within the placement (from start to finish) and from one placement to the next, so that your supervisor can expect both a greater degree of *complexity* and a greater measure of *autonomy* or *self-direction* in a second or third placement. Make sure that you discuss this in the meeting that sets up your placement (▷*Learning Agreement*, 24), and that there is an opportunity very early in the placement to consider what you are bringing with you from the previous placement.

PLACEMENT BRIDGE

We spent a good part of the first supervision session discussing my previous placement. It was helpful for me to remind myself about the ground I'd already covered – it seemed long ago, but it came flooding back. I was impressed that my supervisor had read my portfolio and even made some notes to raise particular points. It made me feel she took my past experiences seriously and it also gave us the chance to talk about the difficulties I'd had with my records and the system they used on my last placement.
Then, when we talked about what I was going to be doing on this placement, it all felt like it fitted in – we could both see how it would connect with my last placement and contrast with it, too.

Shama Bindana, student

At first I was relieved that it was obvious we weren't going over old ground (my previous placement). But it wasn't long before I realised that my supervisor wasn't intersted in stuff I'd already done and didn't know about it. So I found myself repeating stuff and it was like doing my first placement all over again. I wasn't given any credit for being in my last year, so the level of responsibility I was given was no different from my first placement. I thought she'd have known about the trauma I experienced with one of the service users on the first placement but since she didn't raise it (and my tutor didn't at the pre-meeting) I thought I'd better not. But it hung over me like a cloud and made me anxious all the time.

Mary O'Connor, student

As you move from one placement to another you should expect to become more familiar with the student role. Although the second placement is in a new setting, this is not now the first time you have experienced being a student social worker. How is the experience of starting your second or third placement different from starting the previous one? This is no longer your first trip to *Socialworkland* so you should be able to abstract 'the social work' to be able to make links between what might be very different settings and, in making these links, derive an even better understanding of what social work is. Your supervisor, or your off-site practice teacher, is there to help you with this abstraction.

If you failed your previous placement and this is, in fact, a second chance, even more reason to make the placement bridge between the previous and current placement. You are still a relatively experienced student, even if the failed placement has knocked your confidence (▷*Crisis of confidence*, 157).

When students are inexperienced in practice

The regulations for the degree in social work allow young people to begin training straight from school, and some supervisors and tutors voiced concern that this would mean students going on placements with no experience of professional practice. Some students in this situation have noted a reverse ageism – *youthism* – in which their youth is held against them (▷*Unicorns*, 89). Quite apart from the attitude of the supervisor and work colleagues, if you are a young student you might feel self-conscious when working with service users and carers whose life experiences are considerably greater than yours. Expectations of you behaving in a professional manner can feel constraining when you see fellow students on non-professional courses doing what students do.

It is important to return to the chart at the beginning of this chapter, in which you plotted your position and then, more importantly, considered how you can make the best of it and also what you would need to look out for. If you are one of the younger students, you have the advantage of very recently experiencing, and indeed continuing to experience, the greatest life change of all – the journey from childhood to adulthood. Your recent acquaintance with these enormous changes, and reflecting on how you have managed them, can make you especially adaptable and resilient. This can bring tremendous advantages in work with children and young people, whose situations you can perhaps more readily understand (as long as you beware of *over-identification*); also, in work with older people, the generational distance can actually be an advantage.

Be prepared for questions from parents you are working with concerning your own family circumstances ('Have you got children?' etc.) However, these issues of self-disclosure are universal ones, whatever your age as a student and the breadth or narrowness of your life experience. Even the most 'mature' student will encounter people with experiences that lie outside their own, so this is not a situation unique to younger students. It is good practice to see service users as the experts in their own lives and to demonstrate a respect for this, wherever you are on life's journey. Talk openly with your supervisor about how they see your youthfulness and whether they think it will colour their impression of you and your capabilities. Talk openly about any feelings you have of self-consciousness with service users who are older than you. It is always best to have these potential concerns in the open so they can be acknowledged and worked with.

When students are experienced practitioners

The term *student* implies someone who is learning and, in turn, someone who is new to whatever is being studied. However, some people become students after they have practised for many years. They bring considerable experience with them to the programme and they can be a great support to other students who are perhaps studying social work straight from leaving school. In these cases, the social work landscape is already very familiar; indeed, sometimes the student might have spent longer there than the supervisor.

Although this experience comes with some advantages it also creates challenges. 'Wearing L plates' doesn't come easily when you've been driving for so many years. Keeping an open mind when supervisors suggest new ways of doing things and not taking this as an implicit criticism of firmly established habits can be difficult. This might be especially hard when the supervisor is a younger, less experienced person, which is one of the reasons why it is important to discuss your biographies as student and supervisor early on, and reflect on similarities and differences and what you can each learn from this.

Lifelong learning is an overused term, but supervisors who can embrace the reality and not just the rhetoric are good role models for their students. If, as a supervisor, you reflect on your own practices and are open to new ones, this is likely to be an encouragement to the student. In particular, if you follow the *Live teaching* model (▷64) you can create a partnership in which degrees of experience are less significant than learning together and recognising good practice as a lifelong journey of discovery.

Sponsored students

In Chapter 2 we considered how students new to the practice setting might understand their role and explore the student 'boundary' (▷*Student role*, 47). However, what if you are already well known at the practice site, perhaps because you are employed there? (≋1).

Re-Arrival

Some students are sponsored by their employers and are expected to locate their placements there, too. This is quite controversial because a core aspect of a placement is the student's introduction to a to new setting. Assigning you to a placement in the same location as your employment is, certainly, unimaginative. An alternative is to join forces with a neighbouring agency to offer a 'swap' system so that students employed by the one can experience the other with no loss of hours to either organisation (▷*Contrast*, 200).

The challenge for the sponsored student is to create a sense of *re*-arrival. In order to emphasise your changed role, consider taking the *Student boundaries* tour (▷46) with your supervisor – perhaps even with the whole team. It is crucial to create distance between your role as an agency worker and that as a student on placement. Perhaps treat yourself to a new wardrobe to mark the transition!

How to turn a

workplace

into a **placement** *?*

CONTRAST

I was very pleased that I was able to have one of my placements in a different agency from the one in which I worked. At first I'd thought it'd be easier and more comfortable just to carry on in my workplace, but call it a placement. When I heard about the settings the other students on my course were going to and the opportunities they would have I felt pretty jealous. Fortunately, my department had already been in discussions with a neighbouring local authority to see about the prospects for a swap whereby their 'home-grown' students had placements in my workplace and vice versa. Actually, it made me realise how valuable it would be for qualified staff to have these kinds of swaps from time to time because you tend to start to think that the way your agency does things is the only way to do them, and it's a breath of fresh air to go somewhere else.

Brenda Shapiro, student

Halo and horn effects

A further axis could be added to Chart 9.1 ▷193, and that is the extent to which the placement is a new one or one that is experienced in offering practice learning. Many non-traditional placements are relatively new, though by no means all (▷*Credibility over time*, 184). There are advantages to both new and experienced placements, and it is important not to make any assumptions on the basis of how long any particular site has been offering placements.

NOT SO EASY-GOING AS THE LAST ONE

I'd already done a session on the Disability Discrimination Act from the point of view of a wheelchair user and then I was asked to organise an ethnic awareness day. My supervisor said that they always had this day around that time and that students had always taken a lead. The last student had been an African Caribbean man and my supervisor went on about how good he had been –organising different stalls, cooking this and that, getting bands to play, and that he'd been assuming that I'd do one on Asian culture. This limelight role is not what I like. I really didn't want to do it and I wasn't happy about the underlying principles; it seemed a bit tokenistic, 'a taste of India' type of thing. But I felt in a difficult position, especially coming after a lot of issues I'd had to raise about wheelchair access; I just felt that he felt I was trouble. I know that my lukewarm reaction to my supervisor's ethnic awareness day was interpreted as me being awkward again, and somehow not measuring up to all the other past students.

My social network group advised me to talk to my supervisor, not just about the specific thing of the awareness day, but also to share my feelings about being compared. I practised what I was going to say, didn't want him to become all defensive and, actually, he listened to what I had to say and we had a very honest conversation. We're still not what I'd call eye-to-eye, but I think we understand one another a lot better and I don't get the feeling any more that the other students are ghosts in the room like it used to feel.

Shama Bindana, student

Placements in practice sites with a history of students need to learn from this history whilst ensuring that each new student does not feel that they are 'the fourteenth' in line, even though it is inevitable that each student leaves his or her footprint. Sometimes this inheritance is a deliberately planned part of the new student's experience – perhaps the previous student has prepared a welcome pack from the point of view of a student. This kind of handover can be an effective way of acknowledging the student history of the particular placement. More difficult is the legacy of a student who has had an especially strong presence in a placement and leaves a deep imprint, whether this is the halo of an exceptionally able student or the horns of a student who was seen as difficult, for whatever reasons. The current student is likely to hear about these students from others in the team or agency, so it is probably better for these ghosts to be laid to rest quite early on in the placement. The current student will, of course, be wondering what reputation he or she is likely to acquire during the placement.

In Chapter 8 we learned of Shama's experience in a new placement where there was nothing to compare her with (▷*Valuable resource or unpaid labour?* 176). She was pleased to bring 'added value' to that placement, but found this drifting into a sense of being exploited. In *Not so easy-going as the last one* (▷201), Shama considers the same experience, but this time as the latest in a long line of students on placement there.

One other important consideration is the possibility of 'contrast errors' (📚2). This arises when the supervisor's assessment of the current student is founded on a particularly able past student, or even on a standard expected of qualified social workers. This is often not conscious, and supervisors need to remind themselves that the student is a student!

New and experienced supervisors

Four is the magic number

One study found that once supervisors had supported at least four students they demonstrated more confidence in their role, and a stronger commitment to practice education (🖾1). Knowledge that this confidence comes with experience is a key to sustaining motivation and accepting that it is OK to feel awkward in a new role and to have doubts about your own capabilities.

The difficulty in a role that is designated as supervisor or teacher can stem from an assumption that this means you have to know more about everything than your student. This is not – and cannot be – the case. Your student brings new knowledge from their studies that could be valuable to you and your agency as long as you are open to listening. If you are new to supervision you have an affinity with the student, in that you are both setting out on new journeys – the student's to *Socialworkland* itself and you to guiding someone through *Socialworkland*. Of course, there are limits to these parallels: you are in a position of authority and will be making judgements about the student's practice abilities while the student will not be judging your supervisory abilities. The student also wants to feel confidence in you, so there is a fine line between your openness about the newness of the experience on the one hand, and frequent self-disclosures about your self-doubts on the other. It is important to have access to a mentor to whom you can speak freely about any self-doubts and who can help you to develop your skills (▷*Service Agreement*, 27; ▷*Wisdom of the group*, 137).

Experienced supervisors know that each student is different and that even after many placements it is possible to have new challenges to your supervision skills. It is important to find ways of sharing your growing expertise, perhaps through participating in supervisor support groups or teaching on courses, such as *Enabling Others* (▢1), which help to develop others' supervisory skills.

Supervisor as learner

As the supervisor you might actually be a student, engaged in some formal study such as *Enabling Others* (a module designed to help practitioners who are teaching, mentoring or assessing others), working towards a post-qualifying award in practice education or taking an induction course to work-based learning and assessment (☙3). You may wish to record your supervision of the student for your own purposes, perhaps to gather evidence for a portfolio of your supervisory practice. Most students will be very supportive of your study, but it is important to make sure that they know about this beforehand, probably at the pre-placement meeting, when you can explain any formal requirements you have and the implications for the student. It is useful to make a brief record of these in the *Learning Agreement* and/or *Service Agreement* (▷24). The student's anonymity should be guaranteed and they need to be reassured that it does not entail them in any additional assessment – it is your work as supervisor, not theirs as student, that is being collected and assessed for these particular purposes.

APEL, APCL, CATS and ECTS

The guide has tried to avoid acronyms, but the collection that heads this section is hard to avoid. This section explains what each of these terms refers to, and their implications.

If you are an experienced practitioner you may wish to have the learning from your previous experience recognised and 'accredited' so that it can count against the time you need to study. NOTE: Credit cannot be given for practice learning and placement time. APEL stands for *accreditation of prior experience and learning* and refers to a process by which learning achieved outside formal education and training is assessed and recognised (or not) for academic purposes. APCL stands for *accreditation of prior certified learning* and is a similar process to APEL, except that the previous learning *has* been assessed and certified (☜4). Note that it is the *learning* derived from the experience, not the experience in itself that is accredited. This raises the question, how is this learning to be demonstrated? The learning is subject to a standard of *currency* (i.e. the learning must usually have taken place recently, often defined as within the last five years) and only a percentage of the overall credit can be gained in this way. The percentage and time limits vary from programme to programme, so check these out.

If you are wanting to have prior experience accredited, you need to find out how the particular social work programme makes these judgements and the protocols that you will be required to complete, but beware: the demands for an APEL portfolio can be very time-consuming and rigorous (▷*Credit*, 04).

The Credit Accumulation and Transfer System (CATS) enables learners to accumulate credits and transfer them from one institution to another; the European Credit Transfer System (ECTS) allows credits to be traded across

European countries but, rather like shoe sizes, there are still several systems in place, which complicates this kind of transfer. The Bologna agreement is designed to harmonise these systems (⬨2), but current practice is to equate one ECTS credit with two UK credits:

1 ECTS = approx 20 notional hours of learning.
1 UK credit = 10 hours of notional learning.

Research in one region of England showed enormous disparities from course to course, so that moving between universities can be as difficult within a region as between countries (⬚4).

⬨ Click to download

⬨1 'Enabling others effectively: from competence to confidence' (2008), Shropshire Council, NSPCC and University of Wolverhampton:
▷ www.skillsforcare.org.uk

⬨2 For more about the Bologna process:
▷ www.ond.vlaanderen.be/hogeronderwijs/bologna/

⬚ Books, articles, research reports

⬚1 *Strategies concerning work-based learning:*
▷ Downs, S. (1995), *Learning at Work: Effective Strategies for Making things Happen*, London: Kogan Page.
▷ Williams, S. and Rutter, L. (2007), *Enabling and Assessing Work-Based Learning for Social Work: Supporting the Development of Professional Practice*, Learn to Care Publication 10, Birmingham: Learn to Care. www.learntocare.org.uk

⬚2 ▷ Kadushin, A.E. (1992), *Supervision in Social Work*, New York: Columbia University Press.

⬚3 'Induction to work-based learning and assessment in support of the social work degree', produced by the Practice Learning Taskforce / Skills for Care (2005), ▷www.practicelearning.org.uk

⬚4 Research comparing APEL and APCL in post-qualifying social work across an English region:
▷ Aylott, J. and Northrop, P. (2008), *PQ Social Work: APEL and APCL in Yorkshire and the Humber*, Skills for Care, www.skillsforcare.org.uk

CHAPTER TEN

AFTERWARDS

E ven though the placement has ended, the learning from it continues. This chapter considers how to monitor individual placements and the placement provision overall. It considers some of the tensions arising from 'placement dissonance', when the experiences in your placement are at odds with what you have come to expect from the messages in class, or your expectations from a placement are not met in subsequent employment. How can placements be best supported and sustained, and how do your current experiences of placement learning relate to future post-qualifying study?

Links

Background information about your *Fellow travellers* ▷09–11.
More explanation of terms in *Language* ▷226–8.
The following topics have strong links with the themes in this chapter:
▷*Social networking* 74; *Practice panels* ▷143; *From placement to placement* ▷193; *Sustaining placements off the beaten track* ▷182.
Examples of placement documents are indicated by ▷**W**, and can be downloaded at: www.routledge.com/textbooks/9780415499125

Preliminaries

When you start your placement it is not easy to be thinking about *afterwards*, whether afterwards is the period between this placement and the next, or is when you begin your work as a qualified practitioner. However, many of your activities during the placement will stand you in good stead for afterwards, not least your regular entries in a reflective placement diary. More than anything else, this will help you to look back over your time on placement and – like a photograph album – it will give you a sense of what you 'looked like' back then. How have you and your practice changed over that period?

The placement end is a significant event and it is worth considering how you would like to mark this. Much will depend on the culture in the site where you are placed. (Are gifts exchanged? Is there a celebratory meal?) but you should let your supervisor and colleagues know what your preferences would be. Is there likely to be any contact beyond the placement? In most cases this is unlikely, but in some kinds of placement, perhaps where there has been strong advocacy and close relationships, you might maintain a link. It is always useful to begin anticipating the placement end before it suddenly arrives.

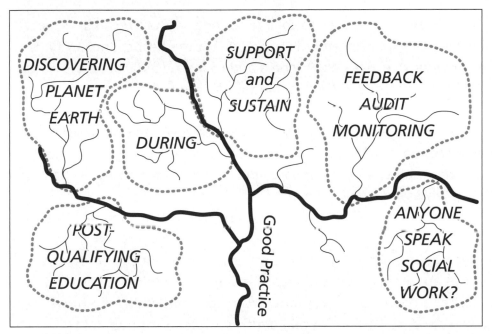

✦ *Chart 10.1: Going with the flow – 'Afterwards' catchment areas*

During

Before we consider what happens after the placement, let us reflect on the *during*. What contact have you had with other students and the programme as a whole during your placement? This will vary considerably from course to course; some have placements that are *concurrent*, which means that part of each placement week is spent at the college or university, whilst others are *block*, with perhaps occasional recall days. These brief returns to class are an important opportunity to check in with other students and find out about their placement experiences, and also to make contact with tutors. One innovative way to help students get the most from these recall days is the 'speed dating' approach (⬚1) described by Sandra Townsend and Nat Davies below. Whatever methods are used, it is important that you are able to get the best out of these occasions, that they enhance your placement experience and that they are not seen as an 'interruption' (▷*Social networking*, 74).

SPEED DATING

When students come back to college for one of their recall days we think very carefully about how to give them the best chance to find out about each other's experiences and to learn from these. We came across a 'speed dating' technique (⬚1), which is a way of students debriefing about the different kinds of agency cultures they've encountered, some of the unwritten rules they've observed, their experiences of supervision and learning, what they've learned about themselves and the impact of placement on the rest of their lives. It works very well.

Sandra Townsend, director of practice studies

The name, 'speed dating' put me off and I was sceptical – I saw the recall as an interruption and wasn't in a frame of mind to respond. But, after a couple of moves (one circle stays put, whilst the other moves round, so you get to talk briefly with loads of people) I started to enjoy it and could see the point of it. I can't think of any other way that I would've got to know so much so quickly about other placements' experiences and it helped me to reflect on my own. There were some people I talked to that I'd not spoken with even when full time in class.

Nat Davies, student

Feedback, audit and monitoring

In Chapter 3 we looked at *Feedback* (▷72) in the context of supervision and live teaching. That is an opportunity to receive one-to-one feedback about your learning and practice, and also to give feedback about your experience of supervision. Another area of feedback focuses on the placement as a whole. Most programmes have pro-formas that invite students, supervisors and other people with an interest in the placement to evaluate their experiences. These are usually collated in order to provide aggregated information about placement provision across individual agencies and also for the social work programme as a whole (▷**W** for an example of a placement feedback form; ▷⊠1).

As with all evaluative feedback there should not be any surprises. The evaluation is not to be used as a chance to vent feelings that have been pent up during the placement. If you have any concerns, irritations or complaints, these should have been discussed responsibly during the placement as they arose. Critical feedback is best given face-to-face, verbally, and at the time rather than later in a written format. You may have found this difficult because of the relative power of the supervisor (in terms of passing or failing your practice), but if you have not been able to find ways of expressing any disagreements or concerns in the supervisor–supervisee relationship, how can you expect to model this form of assertiveness for your service users who might have similar feelings in the face of your power as a social worker?

TIME TO REFLECT

I wondered what the student would have to say because it had been a difficult placement. I hoped he'd feel safe to give honest feedback, but also fair. I liked having the chance to tell about how I found managing the placement. The university makes a decision about whether the placement will be used again and the information in the evaluation is important. I filled my form in, too, and I wrote about the placement as it had been from my experience – not an evaluation of the student, I'd already done that in the report, but more about what I thought about the placement, what made parts of it work well and what parts didn't work so well, and why. There was nothing new, as such, in there, but spending time thinking about it was helpful and I think it was good for the student as well.

John Patterson, service user educator

The final evaluation of the placement should therefore comprise a summary of the regular feedback that has characterised a good placement, and an opportunity to reflect on the experience overall. Of course, critical comment needs to be included, but it should be in the context of this overall reflection, not gripes and criticisms that have not been expressed previously. If you have had less opportunity to give feedback during the placement than you wanted, it is right to note this and how you attempted to redress this *during* the placement. You would rightly feel similarly aggrieved if the first you knew of any criticism of your practice was in the supervisor's final report.

💬 DOOR 1   BE COUNTED?   DOOR 2 💬

The placement had been difficult, largely because of the relative absence of my supervisor, and also because my needs as a disabled student were not properly considered.

DOOR 1	DOOR 2
I was clear about this in the final placement evaluation. I'd raised these issues with the supervisor a number of times and was careful to ask for them to be recorded at the mid-placement review. Some improvements were then made, but towards the end of the placement things started to drift again. I think it's important to have my observations on record so that the agency knows what they need to do if they are to make this a better placement (especially for disabled students) and also so that the university can make a decision about whether to use it again.	*I made some bland comments about the placement and a few hints that it wasn't the best placement ever. It's all very well for the tutors to say they want us to be honest in our feedback but I know different: you get a reputation if you're not careful and it can affect your future employment prospects. So I kept my head down, did nothing to rock the boat and kept my peace, even though I think I was unfairly treated and I don't think this placement should be used again. But why should I stick my neck out?*
Shama Bindana, student	*Shama Bindana, student*

It is useful to think about the purpose of any final evaluation. Is it to record your feedback about your experience of supervision and the placement, so that your supervisor has a formal record of this to keep? Is it to help the placement develop for future students, noting particularly strong aspects and other areas that you feel need strengthening? Or perhaps a reflection on the kinds of student that are likely to benefit most from this particular placement? Of course, the same evaluation can cover all of these purposes and more, but thinking about the potential audience for the feedback helps you to frame it. Feedback is best seen as a kind of gift and, as such, it should be thought about carefully.

Reports of the programme's placement provision overall are also produced on an annual basis, often compiled by the *practice panel* (▷143) and *practice enquiry teams* (▷166). At a national level, all programmes are monitored using Annual Quality Assurance Returns (AQARs) completed by the social work programme against the objectives the programme set itself in the previous year. These returns are collated in England by the General Social Care Council (⊠2). The GSCC does not determine the curriculum or the delivery of the social work degree, but it inspects the quality of social work education against overall content agreed by government. Each programme decides how best to deliver this content and must seek revalidation by the GSCC every five years. Students have the opportunity to take part in this process, usually through the student representatives on the course, as do agencies and service user educators. Placement provision is a significant element in this monitoring and validation, and the quality of information about placements influences the accuracy of the picture that is available.

For all these reasons the monitoring of individual placements and the auditing of placement provision overall are important activities that have significant consequences and should be conducted with care. They should figure in the local and regional workforce plans to ensure that appropriate numbers of social workers are being trained.

Service user feedback

Feedback is a process that we are engaged in all the time. In your direct contact with service users you will have been gauging their responses to your questions, reflections and comments; this verbal and nonverbal communication relies on being responsive to immediate feedback. Reflective feedback results when a little time has passed. This is more difficult to organise with service users, given that your time with them is usually focused on their immediate concerns, not on your performance. However, taking the time at the end of a session to help them reflect on how they have found the *process* of your work together can provide you with helpful advice, as well as demonstrating that you care about their opinion.

HOW WAS IT FOR YOU?

As a sponsored student, one of the strategies to help transform my workplace into a *placement* was for me to become involved in some development work, so that it wasn't too *same-old, same-old*. One of the projects I enjoyed most – though not always at the time, it was a real challenge – was co-leading a group with a colleague from a local voluntary agency. Built in to the group was a pre-test and post-test, basically so that group members could see what changes had occurred as a result of group membership. Also, at the end of every session we would check in to see how people had experienced the group and our leadership of it; in the final session we asked for written feedback – we asked group members to pair up to write their feedbacks (they could disagree with their pair, of course, but I think it made them feel bolder about saying what they wanted to say). I asked permissions to include anonymous copies in my portfolio, which they gave. I learned so much from that group and from the feedbacks – they were very generous, but they also made some comments that made me think and reflect (for example, that some of them had felt a bit threatened by me at the beginning – which came as a real surprise). I'm thinking of ways I can generate this kind of open feedback from my one-to-one work, where feedback tends to be a bit general and 'happy-clappy' if I'm honest.

Brenda Shapiro, student

It is now usually required practice to include formal evaluations from service users in your placement documentation. Having people fill in a questionnaire or respond to a few questions is not difficult; however, achieving this in a way that respects service users' confidentiality, that feels fair to you as student, that is representative of your general practice, and that genuinely gives advice on areas of improvement, is actually quite complex. For this reason, you should review any pro-formas that you will be expected to use with service users, and the arrangements for doing this, and discuss any *tailoring* that you might wish to make with your supervisor. If you follow the model of *direct observation* and *live teaching* (▷63) you will find that seeking written feedback from service users follows rather naturally, since it is part of the process of including them in the fact that you are a learner (⊜2).

Supporting and sustaining placements

We learned earlier how the information from each individual placement can be collated so that the social work programme as a whole learns more about the overall placement provision. For example, what percentage of social workers who are trained to supervise students have done so over the last year? If this is relatively low (perhaps less than 60 per cent), why is this the case and what needs to be done to make better use of this resource? *Practice panels* (▷143) can also take a broader view of the quality of overall placement provision, certainly as it is experienced via the portfolios and reports that come to the panel.

What can we learn from the research into what supports and sustains placements? (▷⊠3; *Sustaining placements off the beaten track*, 182). As long as the placement information is collated systematically and acted on, post-hoc surveys (surveys of placements after they have finished) are a valuable source of data to agencies that have hosted students; they not only provide information about the quality of the practice learning itself, but also give pointers to recruitment and retention issues in the agency (⊠4). In this matter, the personal touch can be very effective, illustrated by some agencies where the director meets students as a group at the end of their placement to see how they have found the experience.

What research we have suggests that practice learning is best sustained when these factors are present:

➤ Strategic approaches to practice learning.
  This helps to root practice learning into the agency's thinking. This approach goes beyond student placements to a wider culture of learning and continuing professional development. One indicator of this is where student supervision is written into the job description for practitioners in the agency.
➤ Reliable information systems that are regularly updated and used.
  An indicator is the agency's knowledge of the percentage of available supervisors who are actively supervising – and its ability to act accordingly on this knowledge (▷LeaRNs, ⌧1).
➤ Broad partnerships with much 'traffic' between the practice site and the educational institution.
  Indicators of this are practitioners' and service users' involvement in planning and delivering elements of the class-based teaching and tutors being engaged in direct practice work (for example, via joint appointments).
➤ Reliable funding.
  This is especially important for small voluntary organisations, since they need reassurance that the time and effort invested in practice learning will continue to attract the resources to sustain it (▷183).

The same research identified some factors that make practice learning difficult to sustain:

➤ Uncertainty around the disaggregation of social work services.
  The energies that go into repeated reorganisation of services mean that there is often little in reserve for activities such as student supervision. A planning blight can descend on an organisation facing a reorganisation or in the midst of or recovering from one.
➤ Confusing terminology and lack of harmonisation between social work programmes.
  There has been a profusion of terms and titles to describe the various roles and activities that in this guide we have termed 'placements' and 'student supervision' (▷Language, 226). This causes confusion which in

turn inhibits study into these activities, because it is difficult to know how to compare like with like when we can't be confident of what, say, 'practice assessor' actually means. Similarly, where social work programmes overlap geographically, it is difficult for practice sites, especially smaller, less well-resourced ones, to manage widely differing documentations and protocols. There is a strong need to harmonise these on a regional basis.

➢ Local autonomy.
Where a team is strongly committed to learning, local autonomy can be very beneficial; however, for an agency developing an expectation that all units offer regular placements, this can be a significant block if some teams are resistant and are able to go their own way.

'Do you speak social work?'

In Chapter 8 we considered the opportunities and potential pitfalls of placements that are off the beaten track, in places where social work is not the main language or possibly not spoken at all (▷*But is it social work?* 173). One of the main challenges there was how you determine what social work is when you are in a setting that is not called social work. Paradoxically, Mary O'Connor found 'real' social work in just this non-social work setting (▷*The ambassador*, 179), to the extent that she internalised a standard for social work practice that she would take with her into future employment wherever that might be. You can imagine that she will be rightly critical of an employment that falls short of this.

What if you are on placement in a setting that *does* purport to 'speak social work', yet the kind of social work that Mary enjoyed is actually missing? That kind of experience can lead to what is sometimes called *cognitive and emotional dissonance*, which basically means a tension between what you think, feel and believe social work to be, and what you experience it to be during your time on placement. In a placement that is off the beaten track you anticipate the need for some interpretation, but finding yourself in a traditional placement where no one 'speaks social work' can be more difficult because you are not prepared for it. Perhaps even more challenging is the discovery in your first employment that the job is not the social work you had come to expect from your placements, even though these constituted half of the time you spent on the course and they were in actual practice settings. Though you should be able to adapt to 'new languages' spoken in the field of social care, it is also important to know what social work is and should be, so that you can exercise proper critical faculties when it is absent or obscured.

Might a whole new professional language, a kind of *Esperanto*, develop out of the new types of worker projects, and what are your thoughts about this? (⊠5)

Newly qualified social worker

The debate about the preparedness of newly qualified social workers for the realities of employment hinges around a fundamental belief about what social work is and should be (⊠6). The experiences of placement can generate expectations that are difficult to fulfill in many social work employments; does responsibility for this lie with the placements or the employments?

Certainly this dissonance has led to complaints by some managers in social work settings that students are not able to 'hit the ground running'. We should at this point remind ourselves that this is an age-old complaint (▷*Hit the ground running?* opposite), and that if it is true, then it is a shared responsibility as students spend half of their time in the practice sites that are noting their unreadiness. Above all, it is necessary to challenge the precept that social work students should be able to 'hit the ground running' as soon as they graduate from their educational courses. Three years is not a long time. It is, rightly, a general education in social work, not a training for a specific job. Of course, the programme should fit newly qualified workers to have the core knowledge, skills and values to be able to learn very quickly how to operate in their new employment, but that is different from being able to do the job immediately. And what 'ground' is it that students are hitting? Would it really be a good use of placement time for you to experience the reality of social work practice by spending more than 40 per cent of your time on administrative work, as one survey showed three-quarters of all social workers to be doing? (🥢3)

HIT THE GROUND RUNNING?

I think I mentioned a while back that I qualified in the 1970s. In my first year as a qualified social worker I had a protected caseload – very protected, actually – and supervision for one and a half hours every week on the dot. We are more than 30 years on and I wish I could say the same is true for every newly qualified social worker now. As an agency I believe we have a responsibility to take the new recruits and nurture their sense of what it is to be a social worker so they can bring these qualities to the particular work that they do in our agency. They can learn fast enough how to fill in our particular assessment forms and operate our computer systems (actually, not that easy!) but I don't think they should be able to 'hit the ground running'. I want to see them questioning our ways of working, calling us to task when they feel that we are not being true to social work values. The best team leaders in the agency encourage this, despite all the pressures. The others complain that the new recruits can't hit the ground running! The interesting thing is, there's no difference in the pressures and workloads of these different team managers – they're all huge – it's really a question of mindset. I don't have to tell you which teams keep a hold of their staff and offer the most placements.

Viv Delaney, practice development manager

As to the significance for the retention of new workers, research into the preparedness of new graduates by their training courses for the realities of practice gives a mixed picture (☜4), perhaps because the importance of this factor varies considerably from one individual to another.

The GSCC's annual report, *Raising Standards: Social Work Education and Training* (☒2) examines the overall picture of social work education and training in England. The 2008 report found that, although the degree is preparing students for the start of their career in social work, the support and ongoing training once they enter the workplace needs to be strengthened. The GSCC also called for social workers to receive a specialist post-qualifying award early in their career to ensure that learning at the degree level is consolidated in practice.

As a newly qualified worker, seek out a mentor. This may or may not be your supervisor or team leader. It should be someone who is experienced and who is practising now in a way that you would like to see yourself practising in a few years' time – this is not just about skill, but also about outlook. Usually this will be someone who retains their enthusiasm for social work, continues to be committed to doing their best with and for service users, and knows how to get the best from the agency, even when this means challenging policies and procedures. Knowing that someone else has made it, and continues to work in ways that are true to the profession's standards and values, can be an inspiration to you in the early years. You need to decide how formal any mentoring might be and make sure that your line manager is on board if the mentor is someone else. If you need back-up for your stance, social exchange theories are considered highly relevant to the retention of staff and mentor arrangements reinforce the richness of these exchanges (☙5).

Post-qualifying education

This guide leaves you at the point of qualification, but it is right to point you in the direction of post-qualifying education. It is not the first thing on your mind when you are busy on your placements, but try to find time to check out what kind of post-qualifying opportunities are available at the site where you are placed, and what colleagues think about them. There is a framework for post-qualifying education (▱7) though agencies differ very widely in the opportunities they make available to their staff. So, it is a good idea to find out how people who are a few years down the line from you are continuing their professional development and making some mental notes about your findings (☙6).

Many of the concepts which you have learned to use during placements – such as the recognition and gathering of evidence, its presentation in a portfolio format, learning diaries and the distinctions between description, analysis and reflection – will be familiar by the time you come to study at post-qualifying level and this will be a great advantage to you.

Discovering 'Planet Earth'

'After all the training and studying we'd done as pilots and engineers to get to the moon safely and back ... what we really discovered was the planet Earth' (⬓7). In preparing for the moon missions nobody had anticipated that the most enduring image of those voyages would be the photograph of our own planet rising above the lunar horizon. Suddenly the place where we spend each passing day was seen in an entirely different perspective, in its entirety for the first time and reflected back to us; and we saw it as something of great beauty and delicacy.

For all the specification of *Learning objectives* (▷24) in your placement plan, there will be unexpected 'photographs', new perspectives like Earth-rise, that have not been anticipated yet can have a dramatic impact on the way you see planet social work. Your 'Discovering Planet Earth' moments might well be the ones that you take most vividly from the placement and into your future practice. It is always important to remember that, though the Learning Agreement is an important roadmap for the coming placement, it is the actual experience of the placement that counts and to allow you to be open to unintended insights.

As a supervisor, too, you can have 'Discovering Planet Earth' moments. Showing someone round a landscape that has grown familiar is one way of seeing it afresh. Students ask the kinds of question you forget to ask, or question your responses in ways that suddenly make you notice things differently. For students and supervisors alike it is best to see your travels in *Socialworkland* as a journey *towards*, and the end of the placement as a staging post, rather than a final destination.

⬓ Click to download

⬓1 The Practice Learning Taskforce developed an audit toolkit, Quality Assurance of Practice Learning (QAPL):

▷ www.practicelearning.org.uk

For audit and evaluation materials drawn from a pilot with seven social work programmes in north-west England, with support from members of the National Organisation for Practice Teaching:

▷ *Quality Assurance Benchmark Statement and Guidance on the Monitoring of Practice Learning Opportunities* (2008) at swd@ skillsforcare.org.uk

It is anticipated that the audit function and quality evaluation questionnaires in the above documents will be incorporated within the LeaRNs national web-based management information system, available to use from September 2009: ▷www.skillsforcare.org.uk

⊡2 The GSCC publishes an annual report looking at the overall picture of social work education and training in England:

Raising Standards: Social Work Education and Training

▷ www.gscc.org.uk/NR/rdonlyres/03DA3D5E-C82D-48A7-A344-C31F4615DDE4/0/Raisingstandards200708Summary.pdf

⊡3 Three research reports published in 2009 throw light on how placements can be supported and sustained:

Sustaining Social Work Practice Learning with Local Authorities;
Revisiting New Approaches to Practice Learning;
How New Projects and Initiatives in Social Work Practice Learning Successfully Mature

▷ www.skillsforcare.org.uk

The Practice Learning Taskforce commissioned a number of research studies which also considered the question of supporting and sustaining practice learning.

These are collected together in the *Capturing The Learning* series:

▷ www.practicelearning.org.uk

⊡4 The links between practice learning, recruitment and retention were researched as part of the Capturing the Learning series:

Effective Practice Learning in Local Authorities (2): Workforce Development, Recruitment and Retention (2006), research by Jonathan Parker and John Whitfield, edited by Mark Doel.

⊡5 ▷ www.cwdcouncil.org.uk or email ntow@cwdcouncil.org.uk

⊡6 The Social Work Task Force was established in 2009 to consider these questions:

➢ How professional social workers are deploying their time now.

➢ Why they prioritise their time in the way they do.

➢ What support and supervision they receive and whether it is effective and fit for purpose.

➢ What actions and behaviours by professional social workers make the most difference to vulnerable children and adults.

➢ How to ensure there are the right number of social workers on the frontline to secure high-quality services and support.

➢ The changes needed to drive improvements in frontline practice.

The first report of the Social Work Task Force:

▷ www.dcsf.gov.uk/swtf/downloads/090505 per cent20Taskforce per cent20LETTER per cent20WITH per cent20ANNEXES.pdf

⊠7 The General Social Care Council's post-qualifying education framework:

▷ www.gscc.org.uk/NR/rdonlyres/C9A2F434-DBA5-4A78-8426-C0304ADF8DC3/0/PQBrochure3.pdf

A UK update on postqualifying social work education:

▷ www.niscc.info/content/uploads/downloads/news/PQ_update_0207.pdf

Books, articles, research reports

≋1 Maidment, J. and Crisp, B.R. (2007), 'Not just for romance: applications of "speed dating" in social work education', *Groupwork*, 17:2, pp13–27.

≋2 An early account of service users' views about student competence:

▷ Baird, P. (1991), 'The proof of the pudding: a study of client views of student practice competence', *Issues in Social Work Education*, 10:1&2, pp24–50.

≋3 A survey of the British Association of Social Workers reported in *Community Care*, 26 April 2007.

≋4 Despite much anecdotal concern, there is mixed evidence from research about the preparedness of new graduates. For example, in the field of child welfare and protection, this study found the issue of preparation to be insignificant:

▷ Samantrai, K. (1992), 'Factors in the decision to leave: retaining social workers with MSWs in public child welfare', *Social Work*, 37:5, pp 454–8.

However, the following study did find it to be important:

▷ Healy, K., Meagher, G. and Cullin, J. (2007), 'Retaining novices to become expert child protection practitioners: creating career pathways in direct practice', *British Journal of Social Work*, published online 13 November 2007, pp1–19

Also:

▷ Bradley, G. (2008), 'The induction of newly appointed social workers: some implications for social work educators', *Social Work Education*, 27:4, pp349–65.

5 Cropanzano, R. and Mitchell, M.S. (2005), 'Social exchange theory: an interdisciplinary review', *Journal of Management*, 31:6, pp874–900. For more on newly qualified social workers:

▷ Keen, S., Galpin, D., Gray, I., Brown, K. and Parker, J. (2009), *Newly Qualified Social Workers: A Handbook for Practice*, Exeter: Learning Matters.

6 The West Midlands Post-Qualifying Consortium conducted regular surveys of post-qualifying experiences:

▷ Rowland, M. (2006), 'West Midlands regional post-qualifying consortium post hoc survey evaluation: 2006', unpublished survey.

A research study into experiences of post-qualifying study:

▷ Doel, M., Nelson, P. and Flynn, E. (2008), 'Experiences of post-qualifying study in social work', *Social Work Education*, 27:5, pp549–71.

Texts on post-qualifying social work practice:

▷ Higham, P. (2008), *Post-Qualifying Social Work Practice*, London: Sage.

▷ Tovey, W. (ed.) (2007), *The Post-Qualifying Handbook*, London: Jessica Kingsley.

7 ▷ Swaaij, L.V. and Klare, J. (2000), *The Atlas of Experience (Scale: Unimaginable; Projection: Subjective)*, the Netherlands: Volcano.

PART THREE

THE

CONTEXTS

A SHORT HISTORY OF PLACEMENTS

The history of social work education is closely linked to the history of social work itself (📚1); training, starting with the first course offered in 1898 at Columbia University, New York, brought with it professionalisation, and 'fieldwork' has always been an important element of this training (though this is less the case in many continental European countries). In the United Kingdom, time spent on placements was fixed at 50 per cent of the programme with the creation of the two-year Diploma in Social Work in 1991 and this percentage was maintained when the minimum qualification was raised to a three-year degree in 2003.

At first, placements were not formalised and the links between what happened in class and what happened in the field were not especially strong. Students were often significant players in developing social work agencies such as the early settlements. Students took an apprenticeship-style role, with judgements about their suitability for social work very largely in the hands of their supervisors when writing the final report.

During the 1980s growing interest in both reflective practice and adult learning theories and methods led to a greater emphasis on *teaching*, with student supervisors in the UK becoming known as *practice teachers*. A National Organisation for Practice Teaching (NOPT) was created, with sister organisations in Scotland (ScOPT) and Wales (WoPT/CAYC). The learning in practice settings began to be conceptualised as a *practice curriculum* – complementing the academic curriculum and of equal standing.

PORTFOLIOS

During the 1990s there was increasing focus on learning as well as teaching, and the notion of *practice learning* became dominant. Students became increasingly responsible for gathering and presenting their own evidence, with the supervisor's report playing a corroborating role. An early experimental project in the use of *portfolios* – an idea borrowed from artists – proved very successful (📚2) and portfolios are now used widely through health and social care placements, though the breadth of materials in the original portfolios (audio and video-tapes, flipchart sheets, etc.) tends to have been lost.

APPROACHES

The 1990s saw somewhat polarised debates between the *competence* approach and the *reflective* approach to practice learning on placements. Broadly, the first focused on students proving their ability to achieve agreed targets and the second put emphasis on the students' capacity for critical thinking and practice, and the broader development of learning organisations. The 2000s saw attempts to reconcile the two approaches, with a growing understanding that practitioners need to be both competent *and* critically reflective.

FUNDING

For most of its history fieldwork has been a grace and favour activity: individual organisations offered a placement as part of their contribution to the education and professional socialisation of the next generation of social workers. During the 1990s in the UK funding was made available to pay 'daily placement fees' and also, from 2003 to 2007, part of

the local authority's grant from central government was dependent on a formula that measured activity in practice learning, brought about by the campaigning of a Practice Learning Taskforce. This brought about a more contractual relationship between universities and *placement providers*.

There continues to be a need to expand the numbers of placements, as student numbers and days on placement have grown. This has resulted in more placements for social work students in non-traditional settings, sometimes where there are no social workers on site. This has been controversial. Where it works well it can enable a resurgence of community social work; where it fails it is usually because there is insufficient support from off-site, trained supervisors.

GENERAL EDUCATION

Social work services in the UK reorganised regularly during the last quarter of the 20th century and continue to do so. Social work finds itself highly specialized, with almost no *generic* social work posts (that is, practitioners working in the community with a broad range of service users often on a neighbourhood basis). Social work education has remained generalist. Even though the practice site is likely to specialise in a particular service user group, the student's course overall is generalist. Students in the UK are expected to experience at least two different kinds of service user group during their education.

Social work educators tend to favour the generalist approach, but there are some political and agency pressures for some specialisation *before* qualification. It is uncertain what the outcome of these pressures will be and the impact of this on placements – and, indeed, on the notion of social work practice in general.

📚1　Chapter 1 of Sheldon, B. and Macdonald, G. (2009) *A Textbook of Social Work*, London: Routledge provides a brief history of social work to set the context for placements.

📚2　Doel, M. and Shardlow, S.M. (1989), 'The practice portfolio: report of an action research project', CCETSW/University of Sheffield.

LANGUAGE

Can you speak *Placement*? It can be a confusing tongue, and it changes over time and from area to area, so here is a rough guide to the language of Placement.

MINDSET

Mental attitudes are important to the success of your placement; your potential for learning is closely linked to your beliefs and attitudes about learning. The guide uses the term mindset to sum up this notion of state of mind.

PLACEMENT

The official term is currently (2009) *practice learning opportunities*, an unwieldy term and one likely to change with the next whim. Day to day, we still hear 'placement' and this is the term the guide uses. It is an abstract concept, referring to the educational experience of social work students outside college.

PRACTICE SITE

'Placement' is the educational experience of social work students outside college; the actual place where the student goes for this experience is the practice site or, sometimes, just *site*. The guide also refers to *on-site* and *off-site* supervision.

PROTOCOLS

Protocols are the pro-formas and templates that are used to collect information in a standard way. An example of a placement protocol is the blank template of the **Learning Agreement**; it enables all students in the programme to supply the same *kind* of information, even though the precise nature of that information will vary from student to student. Practice sites have their own protocols, too (ways of collecting and using recorded information). The **practice portfolio** is a protocol, a template for students to collect evidence of their learning and practice for the purpose of assessment.

SECTORS

Social care is provided by different sectors, which are described according to their funding: the **statutory sector** (state funded), the **voluntary sector** ('not-for-profit'), the **private sector** ('for profit') and the **independent sector**. Together, these last three sectors are sometimes referred to by the

acronym *PVI*. 'Statutory' also refers to the legal functions undertaken by social workers, but these are not restricted to the statutory agencies – some *statutory functions* are undertaken by social workers in voluntary organisations, for example. **Non-traditional placements** are often thought to be those undertaken outside the statutory sector. Though referred to as non-traditional, they probably account for the majority of placements undertaken.

SERVICE USER

People who use the services where the placement is located are known as service users (and sometimes as **self-advocates** or **experts by experience**); their **carers** are involved directly in their care. Service users might also be providing practice learning directly in placements or indirectly through involvement in other parts of the education of students (for example, in the class teaching).

SOCIAL SERVICES

Social services departments in England broke up during the 1990s and 2000s, and there is now no single agency that primarily employs social workers; they are found in **children's services, health** *trusts, adult and neighbourhood services* and many other settings. The guide uses the term *social services* as a collective term for all the services that social workers and social care workers provide.

SUPERVISOR

There is much confusion about the terminology for the people who provide education and training for social work students in practice settings. The guide reverts to the historic term, supervisor. It has the advantage of short simplicity, matching the one-word terms, *student* and *tutor*. Alternatives to supervisor are clumsy, consisting of multiple phrases such as *off-site practice teacher* and *on-site work-based supervisor*. UK government documents refer to *practice assessor*, but the guide does not use this since it privileges one aspect of the role (assessing) and is, therefore, inadequate.

There was good reason for the historic move from the term *student supervisor* to *practice teacher* (▷*A Short History*, 224). However, the teaching and learning functions of practice education are now widely accepted so that, ironically, this gives us confidence to revert to the term *supervisor* in the knowledge that the reader appreciates the full range of implicit activities (▷100–118).

Sometimes the guide employs *practice educator* as a general term for all the people who help students with their practice learning, since *supervisor* implies the main hands-on person. Where there is a need to be very specific, then particular reference is made to, for example, the *on-site supervisor*, the *off-site practice teacher* or *the independent practice educator*.

BOOKS

Adams, R., Dominelli, L. and Payne, M. (eds) (2002), *Social Work: Themes, Issues and Critical Debates* (2nd edition), Basingstoke: Palgrave/Open University Press.

Atherton, S. (2006), 'Putting group learning into practice', West Midlands Learning Resource Network/Skills for Care.

Beverley, A. and Worsley, A. (2007), *Learning and Teaching in*

Social Work Practice, Basingstoke: Palgrave Macmillan.

Bogo, M. and Vayda, E. (1987), *The Practice of Field Instruction*, Toronto: University of Toronto Press.

Bradey, R. (1993), *How To Grow A Social Worker: Tips for Field Teaching* (2nd revised edition), Sydney: University of New South Wales Press.

Bramble, R. (2008), *Aspirations, Encouragement, Realism and Openness: A Guide to Help Increase Children's Happiness and Potential Inside and Outside Schools*, UK: Bramble Jordan.

Brookfield, S.D. (1995), *Becoming a Critically Reflective Teacher*, San Francisco: Jossey Bass.

Brown, A. and Bourne, I. (1996), *The Social Work Supervisor*, Buckingham: Open University Press.

Brown R. and Rutter L. (2006), *Critical Thinking for Social Work*, Exeter: Learning Matters.

Caspi, J. and Reid, W.J. (2002), *Educational Supervision in Social Work: A Task-centered Model for Field Instruction and Staff Development*, New York: Columbia University Press.

Cree, V.E. (ed.) (2003), *Becoming a Social Worker*, London: Routledge.

Cree, V.E. and Davis, A. (2007), *Social Work: Voices from the Inside*, London: Routledge.

Daines, J., Daines, C. and Graham, B. (1998), *Adult Learning, Adult Teaching* (3rd edition), Nottingham: Continuing Education Press.

Doel, M. and Best, L. (2008), *Experiencing Social Work: Learning from Service Users*. London: Sage.

Doel, M., Sawdon, C. and Morrison, D. (2002), *Learning, Practice and Assessment*, London: Jessica Kingsley.

Doel M. and Shardlow S.M. (2005), *Modern Social Work Practice: Teaching and Learning in Practice Settings*, Aldershot: Ashgate.

Doel, M., Shardlow, S.M., Sawdon, C. and Sawdon. D. (1996), *Teaching Social Work Practice: A Programme of Exercises and Activities towards the Practice Teaching Award*, Aldershot: Ashgate.

Downs, S. (1995), *Learning at Work: Effective Strategies for Making things Happen*, London: Kogan Page.

Fletcher, S. (1992), *Competence-Based Assessment Techniques*, London: Kogan Page.

Further Education Development Agency (FEDA) (1995), *Learning Styles*, London: FEDA.

Gould, N. and Taylor, I. (eds) (1996), *Reflective Learning for Social Work*, Aldershot: Ashgate.

Hawkins, P. and Shohet, R. (2007), *Supervision in the Helping Professions* (3rd edition), Berkshire, McGraw-Hill.

Healey, J. and Spencer, M. (2007), *Surviving Your Placement in Health and Social Care: A Student Handbook*, Buckingham: Open University.

Hillier, Y. (2002), *Reflective Teaching in Further and Adult Education*, London: Continuum.

Higham, P. (2008), *Post-Qualifying Social Work Practice*, London: Sage.

Honey, P. (1988), *Face to Face: A Practical Guide to Interactive Skills* (2nd edition) , Aldershot: Gower.

Honey, P. and Mumford, A. (1995), *Using Your Learning Styles* (3rd edition), Berkshire: Peter Honey.

Hunt, G. (ed.) (1998), *Whistleblowing in the Social Services: Public Accountability and Professional Practice*, London: Arnold.

Kadushin, A.E. (1992) *Supervision in Social Work*, New York: Columbia University Press.

Lawson H. (ed.) (1998), *Practice Teaching: Changing Social Work*, London: Jessica Kingsley.

Lishman, J. (2007), *Handbook for Practice Learning in Social Work and Social Care: Knowledge and Theory* (2nd edition), London: Jessica Kingsley.

Lishman J. (ed.) (1994), *Handbook of Theory for Practice Teachers in Social Work*, London: Jessica Kingsley.

Marsh, P. and Triseliotis, J. (1996), *Ready to Practice? Social Workers and Probation Officers: Their Training and First Year in Work*, Aldershot: Avebury.

Minton, D. (2005), *Teaching Skills in Further and Adult Education* (3rd edition), London: Thomson Learning.

Moon, J. A. (2004), *A Handbook of Reflective and Experiential Learning*, Oxon: Routledge Falmer.

O'Hagan, K. (2007), *Competence in Social Work Practice: A Practical Guide for Students and Professionals* (2nd edition), London: Jessica Kingsley.

Parker J. (2005), *Effective Practice Learning in Social Work*, Exeter: Learning Matters.

Payne, M. (2006), *What is Professional Social Work?* (2nd edition), Bristol: Policy Press.

Pritchard, J. (ed.) (1994), *Good Practice in Supervision: Statutory and Voluntary Organisations*, London: Jessica Kingsley.

Reece, I., and Walker, S. (2000), *Teaching, Training and Learning: A Practical Guide* (4th edition), Sunderland: Business Education.

Rogers, J. (2001), *Adults Learning* (4th edition), Berkshire: Open University Press.

Rogers, A. (2002), *Teaching Adults* (3rd edition), Buckingham: Open University Press.

Rogers, A. (2003), *What is the Difference? A New Critique of Adult Learning and Teaching*, Leicester: National Institute of Adult Continuing Education (NIACE).

Royse, D., Dhooper, S.S. and Rompf, E. (2009), *Field Instruction: A Guide for Social Work Students*, New York: Addison Wesley Longman.

Schon, D. (1983), *The Reflective Practitioner: How Professionals Think in Action*, London: Temple Smith.

Shardlow S.M. and Doel M. (1996), *Practice Learning and Teaching*, Basingstoke: Macmillan.

Shardlow S.M. and Doel M. (2002), *Learning to Practise Social Work: International Approaches*, London: Jessica Kingsley.

Shardlow, S.M. and Nelson, P. (eds) (2007), *Introducing Social Work*, Lyme Regis: Russell House.

Sharp, M., and Danbury, H. (1999), *The Management of Failing DipSW Students: Activities and Exercises to Prepare Practice Teachers for Work with Failing Students*, Aldershot: Ashgate.

Sheldon, B. and Macdonald, G. (2008), *A Textbook of Social Work*, London: Routledge.

Smith, A. (1998), *Accelerated Learning in Practice: Brain-based Methods for Accelerating Motivation and Achievement*, Stafford: Network Educational Press.

Thompson, N. (2006), *Promoting Workplace Learning*, Bristol: BASW/Policy Press.

Thompson, N. (2000), *Understanding Social Work: Preparing for Practice*, Basingstoke: Macmillan.

Thompson, S. and Thompson, N. (2008), *The Critically Reflective Practitioner*, Basingstoke: Palgrave Macmillan.

Thompson N., Osada M. and Anderson B. (1994), *Practice Teaching in Social Work* (2nd edition), Birmingham: PEPAR Publications.

Tovey, W. (ed) (2007), *The Post-Qualifying Handbook*, London: Jessica Kingsley.

Trevithick P. (2006), *Social Work Skills: A Practice Handbook* (2nd edition), Maidenhead: Open University Press.

Walker, J., Crawford, K. and Parker, J. (2008), *Practice Education in Social Work: A Handbook for Practice Teachers, Assessors and Educators*, Exeter: Learning Matters.

Walklin, L. (2000), *Teaching and Learning in Further and Adult Education*, Cheltenham: Nelson Thornes.

Yelloly, M. and Henkle, M. (eds) (1995), *Learning and Teaching in Social Work: Towards Reflective Practice*, London: Jessica Kingsley.

INDEX

INDEX OF TRAVELLERS